THE REBIRTH OF AMERICA

Published by
THE ARTHUR S. DEMOSS FOUNDATION

Unless otherwise indicated Scripture quotations are from the *King James Version of the Bible.*

Scripture quotations marked N.I.V. are from *The Holy Bible, New International Version.* Copyright ©1973, 1978, International Bible Society.

Scripture quotations marked J.B. Phillips are from *The Phillips Translation* Copyright © J.B. Phillips 1958, 1960, 1972. Macmillan Publishing Co., Inc.

CONTENTS

SECTION ONE
AMERICA YESTERDAY: A NATION ESTABLISHED

SECTION TWO
AMERICA TODAY: A NATION ADRIFT

SECTION THREE
AMERICA TOMORROW: A NATION REBORN

Appendix

ACKNOWLEDGMENTS

Publisher:	Arthur S. DeMoss Foundation, Philadelphia
Executive Editor:	Nancy Leigh DeMoss
Project Director:	Nelson H. Keener
Written and Compiled by:	Robert Flood
Creative Director:	Mike Johnson
Editorial Assistants:	Ruth Tomczak McClellan Andy Stimer
Research Assistant:	Angela Elwell Hunt
Graphic Design/Production:	The Petragram Group, Virginia Beach

PREFACE

For thousands of years, the eagle has been admired for its grandeur, its grace in flight, and its great size and awesome power.

The soaring eagle is also a stirring picture of the true meaning of liberty.

Assisted by his powerful wings, the eagle glides effortlessly to altitudes of over 2,400 feet and is capable of using his wings to carry other eagles to safety. Turbulent winds only cause him to fly higher and faster.

The eagle's keen eyesight enables him to be sensitive to approaching danger and to protect himself and his family.

The eagle displays the sense of responsibility that is a companion of genuine liberty. He mates for life and returns to the same nest each year, making necessary repairs and additions. He takes an active role in providing for his family and in teaching his young to fly.

In so many ways, the eagle illustrates the life, victory, power, and freedom that Jesus Christ came to give those of us who place our faith in Him.

The eagle also pictures many of those character qualities that made America great and that must be reinstilled in our generation if we are to preserve for our children and grandchildren the freedom which God has so graciously entrusted to us.

My father, Arthur S. DeMoss, was a man of such character. He was a freedom-loving American. And he sought to exercise that freedom responsibly, and to ensure that it would be maintained for subsequent generations.

More than anyone else I have ever known, his life embodied the principles of God's Word. His success in the eyes of the world as an entrepreneur, in the eyes of his family as a devoted husband and father, and in the eyes of heaven as a committed man of God, was a tribute to the value of wholehearted surrender to God and His Word.

Perhaps the most significant accomplishment of his 53 years on this earth, was the spiritual protection, provision, and direction he gave to his wife and seven children. The enduring legacy he left to his family was the conviction that our lives must be lived with the supreme purpose to please God and to radiate the light and truth of His ways to a spiritually dark and needy generation.

Today, his vision and ideals are continuing to be fulfilled through the countless organizations and individuals whose lives he touched. It is with humble gratitude to God that this book is lovingly dedicated to the memory of my godly father, with the prayer that God will raise up in our day a new generation of men, women, and young people who walk with God—men and women who are committed, whatever the cost, to see His righteousness restored in the hearts, homes, and institutions of our land.

NANCY LEIGH DEMOSS
EDITOR

AMERICA YESTERDAY:

A NATION ESTABLISHED

"A nation which does not remember what it was yesterday, does not know what it is today, nor what it is trying to do. We are trying to do a futile thing if we do not know where we came from or what we have been about."   —Woodrow Wilson

Every coin minted in the United States bears, along with the bust of a past hero, these words: LIBERTY—IN GOD WE TRUST. It was not lightly that our forefathers chose these inseparable words, for they knew the tremendous cost and sacrifice that had been paid to secure our freedom. In gratitude, they continually acknowledged that God had made and preserved our nation. They were confident that God was blessing their endeavors because they acknowledged Him and sought His aid in all their doings. They warned future generations that the day God was not earnestly revered in America, she would become a byword among nations.

We would do well today to review their urgent admonitions and the wisdom that was theirs when they forged the greatest and most prosperous nation in all history.

Americans have lost their way in part because they do not know their own Christian heritage. The pages that follow declare that heritage, explain the bedrock foundations of our freedoms, and tell the dramatic story and impact of America's great spiritual awakenings. It is the side of early America that has been either ignored or distorted by the history books.

Several times in the history of our nation widespread revival has put God's people back on course. Each time it has reversed a downward moral trend in society and ultimately unleashed profound social impact.

For in Jesus Christ lie all the secrets of the universe, the origin of life, the direction of history, the life beyond.

Without at least an elementary grasp of God's sovereign hand behind all history, which our founding fathers so clearly understood, modern Americans will overlook the true meaning of their own land.

If many of America's citizens have missed it, then let today's generation know now the mighty sweep of spiritual events in our heritage and the story of how, and when, and why "God shed His grace on thee."

O Beautiful For
Spacious Skies,
For Amber Waves
Of Grain,
For Purple
Mountain Majesties
Above The
Fruited Plain!
America! America!
God Shed His Grace
On Thee
And Crown Thy
Good With
Brotherhood
From Sea To
Shining Sea!

Katharine Lee Bates

MEN WHO PAID FREEDOM'S PRICE

*Our nation's founding fathers knew how to count
the cost of liberty.*

On July 4, 1776, there was signed in the City of Philadelphia one of America's historic documents: the Declaration of Independence. It marked the birth of this nation which, under God, was destined for world leadership.

We often forget that, in declaring independence from an earthly power, our forefathers made a forthright declaration of dependence upon Almighty God. The closing words of this document solemnly declare:

"With a firm reliance on the protection of Divine Providence, we mutually pledge to each other our lives, our fortunes, and our sacred honor."

The fifty-six courageous men who signed that document understood that this was not just high-sounding rhetoric. They knew that if they succeeded, the best they could expect would be years of hardship in a struggling new nation. If they lost, they would face a hangman's noose as traitors.

Of the fifty-six, few were long to survive. Five were captured by the British and tortured before they died. Twelve had their homes, from Rhode Island to Charleston, sacked, looted, occupied by the enemy, or burned. Two

lost their sons in the army. One had two sons captured. Nine of the fifty-six died in the war, from its hardships or from its bullets.

Whatever ideas you have of the men who met that hot summer in Philadelphia, it is important that we remember certain facts about the men who made this pledge: they were not poor men, or wild-eyed pirates. They were men of means; rich men, most of them, who enjoyed much ease and luxury in their personal lives. Not hungry men, but prosperous men, wealthy landowners, substantially secure in their prosperity, and respected in their communities.

But they considered liberty much more important than the security they enjoyed, and they pledged their lives, their fortunes, and their sacred honor. They fulfilled their pledge. They paid the price. And freedom was won.

Someone has said, "To be born free is a privilege. To die free is an awesome responsibility."

Yet freedom is never free. It is always purchased at great cost.

Little did John Adams know how significant his words would be when he spoke to his wife, Abigail, on the passing of the Declaration of Indepen-

15

dence and said, "I am well aware of the toil, and blood, and treasure, that it will cost to maintain this declaration, and support and defend these states; yet, through all the gloom I can see the rays of light and glory. I can see that the end is worth more than all the means."

To those who sacrificed for our freedom, the end was worth the painful means. Where would we, who are citizens of the United States of America, be today if there had not been those who counted the cost of freedom and willingly paid for it? Where will we be tomorrow if men and women of integrity do not come forward today and pay the price to reclaim a dying America?

Posterity—you will never know
how much it has cost my generation
to preserve your freedom. I hope
you will make good use of it.
JOHN QUINCY ADAMS

What we obtain too cheaply, we
esteem too lightly; it is dearness only
that gives everything its value.
Heaven knows how to put a price upon
its goods, and it would be strange
indeed if so celestial an article as
freedom should not be highly rated.
THOMAS PAYNE, 1776

For the support of this declaration,
with a firm reliance on the protection
of the Divine Providence, we mutually
pledge to each other, our lives, our
fortunes, and our sacred honor.
DECLARATION OF INDEPENDENCE

ONE NATION UNDER GOD

BY RUS WALTON

*Our very political superstructures stand upon
the critical bedrock of cherished biblical principles.*

In the beginning...
   At the point in God's good time when the Constitutional Convention had completed its work...
   The lady sidled up to old Ben Franklin.
   "Well, Dr. Franklin. What have you given us?"
   "You have a republic, madame. If you can keep it."
   There had been other governments before that had gone by that description—that word, "republic."
   But those were different. Different in origin. Different in nature. Different in structure. The best of that past was incorporated into this new and true republic. The rest—the evil, the excess—was rejected.
   So this new creation stood unique. A system of self-government. By the consent of the governed. And, with union.
   A constitutional republic with individual liberty, elected representatives and limited government. A government with its powers nailed down; fastened and confined to the proper defense of the individual—to his pursuits of life, liberty, property and

happiness, those inalienable rights endowed by The Creator.
   A republic in which the power to govern was checked and balanced by devices designed to stop the tyrant in his tracks.
   The sons of liberty joined to erect four fences around their government, so it could not get out of hand or out of bounds: The Executive, the Legislative, the Judicial, and the Individual. Each was to be a check, or balance, on the other.
   After God, the individual came first. Only by his consent could government govern—and then, only to protect his life, liberty and property. Not just his, but all men—equally.

The New Nation: A Republic, Not a Democracy.

   And so the founding fathers created a republic.
   A democracy? Where half plus one can squash the rest? Where a fanatical majority can deprive the individual of his rights, his life, his property? Not for these men.
   They knew democracy with its excesses, its leveling-down process, its

Ruins at Jamestown

inherent seeds of destruction. They knew Plato's warning that unrestricted democracy must result in a dictatorship.

The very essence of democracy rests in the absolute sovereignty of the majority. Our founding fathers could never accept such tyranny. They recognized only one rightful sovereign over men and nations—not the state, not the majority.

"Each religion has a form of government, and Christianity astonished the world by extablishing self-government...the foundation stone of the United States of America."[1]

But our founding fathers realized the impossibility of maintaining freedom unless those who are "at liberty" are able to exercise self-restraint.

And they gave to this government just enough power to serve. Just enough and no more.

And even then, with all the checks and balances and fences of that constitutional document, it was not until the Bill of Rights was tacked on that the states consented to the union and ratified the federation.

A New Ideal: Freedom of Religion, Not from Religion.

Christ died—and rose—to make men free. All men, all nations.

Through Christ we are freed from the wages and the death of sin. Eternal freedom.

Free from the ravages of appetite. Internal freedom. If we choose to be.

Free from the savagery of dema-

gogues and kings. External freedom. If we choose to be.

Just as Christ brought us internal freedom (and a rebirth into a new life through Him) so He brought us a new direction for our external freedom (and a new purpose for our civil government).

If Christ would die for men, where did Ceasar get off forcing men to live—and die—for him?

There! There was the spark, the flame, the beacon light of the American idea. The power of the great American republic. The sense of the Constitution of these United States.

The Constitution Was Designed To Perpetuate A Christian Order.

"The concept of a secular state was virtually non-existent in 1776 as well as in 1787, when the Constitution was written, and no less so when the Bill of Rights was adopted. To read the Constitution as the charter for a secular state is to misread history, and to misread it radically. The Constitution was designed to perpetuate a Christian order."[2]

Why then is there, in the main, an absence of any reference to Christianity in the Constitution?

Because the framers of the Constitution did not believe that this was an area of jurisdiction for the federal government. It would not have occurred to them to attempt to re-establish that which the colonists had fought against, namely, religious control and establishment by the central government.

"The freedom of the first amendment from federal interference is not from religion but for religion in the constituent states."[3]

Separation of church and state? Absolutely!

Divorcement of God from government? Not so!

The American system is the political expression of Christian ideas...a nation founded upon the rock of religion and rooted in the love of man.

In 1851, when Daniel Webster was reviewing the history of "this great American family," he reaffirmed the need and role of God in government:

"Let the religious element in man's nature be neglected, let him be influenced by no higher motives than low self-interest, and subjected to no stronger restraint than the limits of civil authority, and he becomes the creature of selfish passion or blind fanaticism."

"On the other hand, the cultivation of the religious sentiment represses licentiousness...inspires respect for law and order, and gives strength to the whole social fabric, at the same time that it conducts the human soul upward to the Author of its being."

More than one hundred years after Webster, Charles Malik, one-time Ambassador to the United Nations from Lebanon, put it this way:

"The good (in the United States) would never have come into being without the blessing and the power of Jesus Christ...I know how embarrassing this matter is to politicians, bureaucrats, businessmen and cynics: but, whatever these honored men think, the irrefutable truth is that the soul of America is at its best and highest, Christian."

Our laws and our institutions must necessarily be based upon and embody the teachings of The Redeemer of mankind. It is impossible that it should be otherwise; and in this sense and to this extent our civilization and our institutions are emphatically Christian...This is a religious people. This is historically true. From the discovery of this continent to the present hour, there is a single voice making this affirmation...we find everywhere a clear recognition of the same truth...These, and many other matters which might be noticed, add a volume of unofficial declarations to the mass of organic utterances that this is a Christian nation.

SUPREME COURT DECISION, 1892.
CHURCH OF THE HOLY TRINITY V. UNITED STATES.

WHAT'S SO GREAT ABOUT AMERICA?

What lies behind an abundance unprecented in history, and freedoms which are the envy of the world?

Half the world goes to bed hungry. And half the world lies under Communist rule, where freedom, as Americans know it, simply does not exist.

Homemakers in much of the world might never see in a lifetime the quantity of food which the American housewife can choose in just one trip to the supermarket.

Is this abundance and this freedom ours merely by chance?

Is it wholly due to what Americans like to perceive as U.S. energy and know-how?

If God indeed has blessed America, why?

The Greatness of America's Land.

Some say the land itself has made America great.

One of our most moving patriotic hymns cites the beauty of America—a beauty that all who have traveled across the continent surely recognize. Katherine Lee Bates stood atop Pike's Peak and scanned the sweep of the land, then wrote of the "purple mountain majesties," and the "amber waves of grain." She concluded that God had shed His grace on this land—a vast unexplored wilderness that, in an astonishingly short period, grew into a great nation.

It would be foolish to deny that the rich natural resources of the land itself have not helped to make America. The oil, the ore, the timber, the water, the soil and climate, all have combined to nourish a civilization that would eventually spread from sea to shining sea.

Other nations too, though, have been blessed with fine resources: yet somehow these have not risen to such greatness.

The Greatness of America's People.

Others have said that America's people have made her great. Lyman Abott once said:

"A nation is made great, not by its fruitful acres, but by the men who cultivate them: not by its great forests, but by the men who use them; not by its mines, but by the men who build and run them. America was a great land when Columbus discovered it: Americans have made of it a great nation."

And so they have. For they pioneered a continent, subdued the elements that at first worked against them, molded a society of peoples from all over the world. America's initiative and ingenuity are known across the earth. Other nations have looked on in awe at her ability over the decades to produce not only her own needs, but much more.

The Greatness of America's System.

America's free enterprise system and the spirit of her people, it would seem, have combined to deliver a flood of mass-produced goods to the consumer at relatively low cost. At the same time, American economic genius has also helped to produce millions of jobs— from the factories to the professions— which give Americans the income to buy the goods they produce.

The Greatness of America's Generosity.

Thus far America has escaped the spectre of widescale hunger at home, and she has been able to feed at least some of the hungry abroad. Through the decades she has opened her heart to the poor of the world. She has given generously to every nation, even her enemies, in time of emergency.

The Greatness of America's Freedoms.

In spite of certain social ills, the U.S. has passed more social legislation and enacted more laws providing individual liberty than any other nation in world history. And because of her belief in freedom of speech she has not hidden her scars—they are there for the world to see—while those totalitarian regimes that run a controlled press look on amazed.

All of these blessings point back to her foundations and to the providential hand of God. After all, the purple mountain majesties and the fruited plains originated with God. America's blessings, despite her ills, call forth thanksgiving from all those who enjoy them. The great spiritual heritage that built America unfolded by remarkable design. So also did American democracy, the U.S. Constitution and, along with these, the great freedoms they ensure.

No, America, did not just happen by chance, as is obvious to a person who truly understands the unfolding saga of events that shaped this nation. The pages that follow highlight some of this evidence, not that we should simply look back, but that we should better understand where America is today, how she arrived here, and where she must turn at this critical hour.

For as Thomas Jefferson once asked, "Can the liberties of a nation be secure, when we have removed the conviction that these liberties are the gift of God?"

My God! how little do my
countrymen know what precious
blessings they are in possession of, and
which no other people on earth enjoy!

THOMAS JEFFERSON

PLYMOUTH ROCK: A FIRM FOUNDATION

When the Mayflower landed at Plymouth Rock, Christians laid the foundations for a republic that would endure through the centuries.

When Americans look back to their beginnings, they usually point to the little band of sea-weary pioneers that landed in 1620 at Plymouth Rock. Of the more than one hundred Pilgrims aboard the Mayflower, the majority were devout Christians. They were Separatists bent on shaking the Church of England and building a new life in an unknown wilderness, where they could worship the Lord in the way they believed the Scriptures taught.

The Pilgrims: Law and Order for a New Land.

Halfway across the Atlantic, the Mayflower and her crew faced near disaster in a terrific storm that caused one of the main beams to bow and crack. Although the passengers and crew wanted to turn back, Christopher Jones, the ship's Master, assured all that the vessel was "strong and firm under water." He ordered the beam to be secured. It was hoisted into place by a great iron screw that, fortunately, the Pilgrims brought out of Holland. Upon raising the beam, they "committed themselves to the will of God and resolved to proceed."

The battered ship finally came within sight of Cape Cod on November 19, 1620. The Pilgrims scanned the shoreline just to the west of them and described it as "a goodly land wooded to the brink of the sea," which was true of Cape Cod at that time. But they had no patent to sanction their going ashore at Cape Cod, for their charter had been issued for the Virginia Colony—still to the south. This was "no man's land."

The ship moved out into the deep water again while her occupants pondered what to do. Their decision: the Mayflower Compact. It was intended only as a temporary pact to keep the law and order among themselves in a wilderness where there was no law. Yet that historic agreement laid the foundations of law and order and established the first "civil body politic" in America.

At the heart of the compact lay an undisputed conviction that God must be at the center of all law and order and that law without a moral base is really no law at all.

The compact also rested on a "covenant" agreement and this too would later help lay the foundations of the American republic. All law, they insisted, would rest not upon a monarchy or a dictatorship, but upon "the consent of the governed." It was a revolutionary concept for its time.

The day the Pilgrims signed the Mayflower Compact, according to their own historian, William Bradford, "they came to an anchor in the Bay, which is a good harbor...compassed about to the very sea with pines, juniper, sassafras and other sweet wood...." And there, said Bradford, recounting the event several years later, they "blessed the God of heaven, who had brought them over the fast and furious ocean... and a sea of troubles before. 'Let them, therefore, praise the Lord, because He is good and His mercies endure forever.' " (Scripture quoted from the *Geneva Bible* used by the Pilgrims.)

The Puritans: Moral and Academic Education for a New People.

While the Pilgrims carved out their own niche in American history, they were a tiny lot alongside the swarm of Puritans who crossed the ocean and settled along the shores of Massachusetts Bay in the 17th Century.

Like the Pilgrims, the Puritans stood at odds with the Church of England and its hierarchy. In their eyes the Reformation in Europe had not gone far enough. But unlike the Pilgrims, who were strong separatists, they were not yet ready to "pull out." Instead, they wanted to continue the reformation from within and strive for a "pure" church. The wild American continent gave them a chance to escape the corruptions they saw in their own church-state homeland.

John White of Dorchester started the movement to America. He set out to establish a commercial fishing company and, at the same time, to minister to the English fishermen who were beginning to work the New England waters. The company failed, but White promptly saw the opportunity for Christians to establish a colony on new soil where they could model society along biblical lines.

In 1629 England's King Charles granted the Puritans a charter for the Massachusetts Bay Company. Since the goal was religious, and no longer a business venture, why did he allow it?

Some have suggested that the king was more than glad to send some of his sharpest critics three thousand miles across the ocean! Whatever the case, again the divine hand of Providence seemed to be molding America.

By little more than a decade later, some 20,000 colonists had made their way across the Atlantic to New England. Many of these were not Puritans. In fact, perhaps less than one-fifth even professed to be Christians.

But it was the Puritan Christians who established the goverment, built the schools, administered the churches and set the moral tone.

Puritan New England strongly helped shape the foundations of the nation to come. Men like John Cotton and Increase Mather preached forcefully from her pulpits.

What the early Puritans gave American culture, says one observer, amounts to much more than the "blue laws" and

The Divine Hand of Providence Seemed To Be Molding America.

the religious discipline which critics like to caricature.

The Puritans established education in the New England colonies. They gave us a thoroughgoing respect for learning, our first books, our first college, and the habit of representative government.

Lastly, our ancestors established their system of government on morality and religious sentiment. Moral habits, they believed, cannot safely be trusted on any other foundation than religious principle, nor any government be secure which is not supported by moral habits.

DANIEL WEBSTER

A Pilgrim Thanksgiving

EVIDENCES OF OUR CHRISTIAN HERITAGE

There are many evidences that our nation was founded on a commitment to God and the principles of His Word.

In the summer of 1787, representatives met in Philadelphia to write the Constitution of the United States. After they had struggled for several weeks and had made little or no progress, eighty-one-year-old Benjamin Franklin rose and addressed the troubled and disagreeing convention that was about to adjourn in confusion.

"In the beginning of the contest with Britain, when we were sensible of danger, we had daily prayers in this room for Divine protection. Our prayers, Sir, were heard and they were graciously answered. All of us who were engaged in the struggle must have observed frequent instances of a superintending Providence in our favor...Have we now forgotten this powerful Friend? Or do we imagine we no longer need His assistance?

"I have lived, Sir, a long time, and the longer I live, the more convincing proofs I see of this truth: that God governs in the affairs of man. And if a sparrow cannot fall to the ground without His notice, is it probable that an empire can rise without His aid? We have been assured, Sir, in the Sacred Writings that except the Lord build the house, they labor in vain that build it. I firmly believe this...

"I therefore beg leave to move that, henceforth, prayers imploring the assistance of Heaven and its blessing on our deliberation be held in this assembly every morning."

The very purpose of the Pilgrims in 1620 was to establish a government based on the Bible. The New England Charter, signed by King James I, confirmed this goal: "... to advance the enlargement of Christian religion, to the glory of God Almighty...."

Governor Bradford, in writing of the Pilgrims' landing, describes their first act: "being thus arrived in a good harbor and brought safe to land, they fell upon their knees and blessed the God of heaven..."

Confirmed by the Colonies.

The goal of government based on Scripture was further reaffirmed by individual colonies such as The Rhode Island Charter of 1683 which begins: "We submit our persons, lives, and estates unto our Lord Jesus Christ, the King of kings and Lord of lords and to all those perfect and most absolute laws of His given us in His Holy Word." Those "absolute laws" became the basis of our Declaration of Independence, which includes in its first paragraph an appeal to the laws of nature and of nature's God. Our national Constitution established a republic upon the "absolute laws" of the Bible, not a democracy based on the changing whims of people.

Reaffirmed by the Presidents.

In his inaugural address to Congress, the first president of our nation stressed God's role in the birth of this republic:

"No people can be bound to acknowledge and adore the invisible hand which conducts the affairs of men more than the people of the United States. Every step by which they have advanced to the character of an independent nation seems to have been distinguished by some token of providential agency...We ought to be no less persuaded that the propitious smiles of heaven cannot be expected on a nation that disregards the eternal rules of order and right, which heaven itself has ordained."

One of George Washington's early official acts was the first Thanksgiving Proclamation, which reads, "Whereas it is the duty of all nations to acknowledge the providence of Almighty God, to obey

George Washington

his will, to be grateful for his benefits, and humbly implore His protection and favor...." It goes on to call the nation to thankfulness to Almighty God.

Continuing through the decades of history, we find in the inaugural addresses of all the Presidents, and in the Constitution of all fifty of our states, without exception, references to the Almighty God of the universe, the Author and Sustainer of our liberty.

Observed by Historians.

The principles of God's Word guided the decisions on which this nation built its foundation. This was the discovery of Alex DeTocqueville, the noted French political philosopher of the nineteenth century. He visited America in her infancy to find the secret of her greatness. As he traveled from town to town, he talked with people and asked questions. He examined our young national government, our schools and centers of business, but could not find in them the reason for our strength. Not until he visited the churches of America and witnessed the pulpits of this land "aflame with righteousness" did he find the secret of our greatness. Returning to France, he summarized his findings: "America is great because America is good; and if America ever ceases to be good, America will cease to be great."

Throughout our history, our forefathers have given eloquent testimony of our commitment to God and His principles:

"It is the duty of nations, as well as of men, to own their dependence upon the overruling power of God and to recognize the sublime truth announced in the Holy Scriptures and proven by all history, that those nations only are blessed whose God is the Lord."
Abraham Lincoln

"The religion which has introduced civil liberty is the religion of Christ and His apostles...to this we owe our free constitutions of government."

Noah Webster

The concluding words of our National Anthem summarize the fact that the United States of America was born out of a commitment to God and His principles.

"Blessed with victory and peace, may
    this Heav'n-rescued land
Praise the Power that hath made and
    preserved us a nation!
Then conquer we must, when our
    cause it is just;
And this be our motto: 'In God is our
    trust!'
And the star-spangled banner in
    triumph shall wave
O'er the land of the free, and the home
    of the brave."

⚜

The moral principles and precepts contained in the Scriptures ought to form the basis of all our civil constitutions and laws. All the miseries and evils which men suffer from vice, crime, ambition, injustice, oppression, slavery, and war, proceed from their despising or neglecting the precepts contained in the Bible.

NOAH WEBSTER

THE BIBLE AND THE DAWN OF THE AMERICAN DREAM

BY JOHN W. WHITEHEAD

When the Reformation swept over Europe, it put the Bible in the hands of the people, revolutionized concepts of government and set the stage for the American Republic. With the influence of Samuel Rutherford, John Witherspoon and John Locke, the Bible became the basis of United States government and law.

The Reformation in Europe revolutionized concepts of government. It provided the framework for political freedom unknown up to that time. The standard of reference, the Bible, was placed in the hands of the people. Freedom could exist without license and without chaos. The event led to a culture that brought about the civil freedoms and benefits Western Europe and the United States have enjoyed for centuries.

Christian theism teaches that man is held accountable to his Creator. Absolute standards exist by which all moral judgments of life are to be measured. With the Bible, there is a standard of right and wrong.

Rutherford: Government based on God.

These fundamental principles made up the Reformation world view. They were passed on in substance and without significant alteration to the American colonies through the influence of a book written by a Presybterian minister, Samuel Rutherford, *Lex, Rex* or, *The Law*

and the Prince (1644).

Lex, Rex challenged the fundamental principle of seventeenth-century political government in Europe: the divine right of kings. Rutherford asserted that the basic premise of government and, therefore, of law must be the Bible, the Word of God rather than the word of any man. All men, even the king, Rutherford argued, were *under* the law and not above it.

Locke, Witherspoon: The Declaration of Independence and the Constitution.

Though Rutherford died before his concepts were implemented, his ideas lived on to influence later generations. His basic presupposition of government based upon the absolutes of the Bible was finally realized in colonial America through the influence of John Witherspoon and John Locke.

Witherspoon, a Presbyterian minister who had been educated at Edinburgh University,

John Witherspoon

God's Word, the basis for government and law depicted by the fresco in the old Supreme Court Building in Lausanne, Switzerland, is titled, "Justice Lifts the Nation."

brought the principles of *Lex, Rex* into the writing of the Constitution. He was the only clergyman to sign the Declaration of Independence.

Dr. Francis Schaeffer has noted that many "of the men who laid the foundation of the United States Constitution were not Christians in the full sense, and yet they built upon the basis of the Reformation either directly through the *Lex, Rex* tradition or indirectly through Locke." Our political institutions have their base in their Reformation thinking.

Blackstone: The Divine Origin of Rights and Laws.

The renowned, eighteenth-century English jurist, William Blackstone also played a leading role in forming a Christian presuppositional base to early American Law. Blackstone's ideas on law were readily accepted in the colonies.

A lecturer at law at Oxford, he embodied the tenets of Judeo-Christian theism in his *Commentaries.* In the first century of American independence, the *Commentaries* were not merely an approach to the study of the law; for most lawyers they constituted all there was of the law.

William Blackstone

Blackstone, a Christian, believed that the fear of the Lord was the beginning of wisdom. Thus he opened his *Commentaries* with a careful analysis of the law of God as revealed in the Bible.

Blackstone took it as self-evident that God is the source of all laws, whether they were found in the Holy Scriptures or were observable in nature. His presuppositions were thoroughly Christian, founded upon the belief that there existed a personal, omnipotent God who worked in and governed the affairs of men. In consequence, man was bound by those laws, which were in turn a system of absolutes.

In Blackstone's view, and in the eyes of those who founded the United States, every right or law comes from God, and the very words *rights, laws, freedoms,* and so on are meaningless without their divine origin.

Blackstone's influence is clearly expressed in the Declaration of Independence. The colonists argued that it is "the Laws of Nature and of Nature's God" that entitled them to independence and to an equal station among nations. In echoing *Lex, Rex* the colonists proclaimed that "all men are created equal."

The Judeo-Christian Basis of American Law.

In seeking independence from Great Britain the colonists declared to the world their belief in a personal, infinite God—"their Creator"—who endowed them with "certain inalienable" or absolute rights.

To the men of that time, it was self-evident that if there were no God there could be no absolute rights. Unlike the French revolutionaries a few years later, the American colonists knew very well that if the inalienable rights they were urging were not seen in the context of Judeo-Christian theism, they were without content.

The Declaration of Independence, therefore, is structured upon a Judeo-Christian base in two fundamental ways.

First, it professes faith in a "Creator" who works in and governs the affairs of men in establishing absolute standards to which men are held accountable.

Second—and even more fundamentally, since all Western nations of that era professed a belief in the Creator—there is the idea that man is a fallen creature and, hence, cannot be his own lawgiver and judge.

In the end it is God to whom the appeal must be made. In this sense, the law cannot be simply what a judge or a fuhrer says it is. It is what God says it is.

The first and almost the only Book
deserving of universal attention is the Bible.
JOHN QUINCY ADAMS

All the good from the Saviour of the world
is communicated through this Book;
but for the Book we could not know right
from wrong. All the things desirable to
man are contained in it.
ABRAHAM LINCOLN

...the Bible...is the one supreme source of
revelation of the meaning of life, the nature
of God and spiritual nature and need of men.
It is the only guide of life which really leads
the spirit in the way of peace and salvation.
WOODROW WILSON

Go to the Scriptures...the joyful promises it
contains will be a balsam to all your troubles.
ANDREW JACKSON

The foundations of our society and our
government rest so much on the teachings of
the Bible that it would be difficult to support
them if faith in these teachings would cease to
be practically universal in our country.
CALVIN COOLIDGE

WHEN AMERICA CRIED FOR BIBLES

*Even the U.S. Congress cleared a printing
of Bibles, and American statesmen helped spread
them throughout the land.*

The American Revolution was in full swing. The Bible, through more than one hundred fifty years of early settlement in America, remained the base of her people's religious devotion, her education, her colonial government. These Bibles had been shipped in from England.

Now, suddenly the American Revolution cut off this supply, and the stock dwindled.

Here was America in its greatest crisis yet—and without Bibles! Patrick Allison, Chaplain of Congress, placed before that body in 1777 a petition praying for immediate relief. It was assigned to a special committee which weighed the matter with great care, and reported:

"...that the use of the Bible is so universal and its importance so great that your committee refer the above to the consideration of Congress, and if Congress shall not think it expedient to order the importation of types and

paper, the Committee recommend that Congress will order the Committee of Congress to import 20,000 Bibles from Holland, Scotland, or elsewhere, into the different parts of the States of the Union.

"Whereupon it was resolved accordingly to direct said Committee to import 20,000 copies of the Bible." During the session in the fall of 1780 the need arose once more.

Robert Aitken, who had set up in Philadelphia as a bookseller and publisher of *The Pennsylvania Magazine,* saw the need and set about quietly to do something about it.

In early 1781 he petitioned Congress and received from them a green light to print the Bibles needed. The Book came off the press late next year, and Congress approved it.

So originated the "Bible of the Revolution," now one of the world's rarest books—the first American printing.

HOW CHRISTIANS STARTED THE IVY LEAGUE

Harvard, Yale, Princeton, Dartmouth—all owe their origins to the Christian gospel.

Probably no segment of American higher education has turned out a greater number of illustrious graduates than New England's Ivy League. Labels like Harvard, Yale, Princeton, still carry their own mystique and a certain aura of elitism and prestige.

Yet perhaps it would surprise most folk to learn that almost every Ivy League school was established primarily to train ministers of the gospel—and to evangelize the Atlantic seaboard.

Harvard, 1638.

It took only eighteen years from the time the Pilgrims set foot on Plymouth Rock until the Puritans, who were among the most educated  people of their day, founded the first and perhaps most famous Ivy League school. Their story, in brief, is etched today in the record of Harvard:

Harvard

"After God had carried us safely to New England, and we had built our houses, provided necessaries for our livelihood, reared convenient places for God's worship, and settled the civil government; one of the next things we longed for, and looked after was to advance learning, and perpetuate it to posterity; dreading to leave an illiterate ministry to the churches, when our present ministers shall lie in the dust."

Harvard College's first presidents and tutors insisted that there could be no true knowledge or wisdom without Jesus Christ, and but for their passionate Christian convictions, there would have been no Harvard.

Harvard's "Rules and Precepts" adopted in 1646 included the following essentials:

"Every one shall consider the main end of his life and studies to know God and Jesus Christ which is eternal life.

"Seeing the Lord giveth wisdom, every one shall seriously by prayer in secret seek wisdom of Him.

"Every one shall so exercise himself in reading the Scriptures twice a day that they be ready to give an account of their proficiency therein, both in theoretical observations of languages and logic, and in practical and spiritual truths...."

According to reliable calculation, fifty-two percent of the seventeenth-century Harvard graduates became ministers!

Yale, 1701.

By the turn of the century

Yale

Christians in the Connecticut region launched Yale as an alternative to Harvard. Many thought Harvard too far away and too expensive, and they also observed that the spiritual climate at Harvard was not what it once had been.

Princeton, 1746.

This school, originally called "The College of New Jersey," sprang up in part from the impact of the First Great Awakening. It also retained its evangelical vigor longer than any other Ivy League schools. In fact,

Princeton

Princeton's presidents were evangelical until at least the turn of the Twentieth Century, as also many of the faculty.

Dartmouth, 1754.

A strong missionary thrust launched this school in New Hampshire. Its royal charter, signed by King George III of England, specified the school's intent to reach the Indian tribes, and to educate and Christianize

Dartmouth

English youth as well. Eleazar Wheelock, a close friend of evangelist George Whitefield, secured the charter.

Columbia, William and Mary, and other Christian Colleges.

The first president of New York's *Columbia University,* first known as "King's College," at one time served as a missionary to America under the English-based "Society for the Propaga-

tion of the Gospel in Foreign Parts."

The Church of England established the *College of William and Mary,* near today's Colonial Williamsburg. Dutch Reformed revivalists founded *Queen's College* (later Rutgers University) in New Jersey. *Brown University* originated with the Baptist churches scattered on the Atlantic seaboard.

William and Mary

With the exception of the University of Pennsylvania, every collegiate institution founded in the colonies prior to the Revolutionary War was established by some branch of the Christian church.

Even at Penn, however, an evangelist played a prominent part. When Philadelphia churches denied George Whitefield access to their pulpits, forcing him to preach in the open, some of Whitefield's admirers, among them Benjamin Franklin, decided to erect a building to accommodate the great crowds that wanted to hear him. The structure they built became the first building of what is now the University of Pennsylvania, and a statue of Whitefield stands prominently on that campus today.

Though the Ivy League schools eventually turned secular, they fed into the mainstream of society in those earlier days a great army of graduates who could claim Jesus Christ as personal Saviour and Lord, and who left a strong impact on our nation. Their presidents and their faculties helped to set a high spiritual tone, and at times their campuses in turn felt the impact of revival. The educators of early America understood clearly that the moral climate of its schools, colleges and universities would shape its future generations, and could ultimately decide the course of the nation.

THE REBIRTH OF AMERICA

ALL WHO HAVE
MEDITATED ON THE ART
OF GOVERNING
MANKIND ARE
CONVINCED THAT
THE FATE OF EMPIRES
DEPENDS ON THE
EDUCATION OF YOUTH.

ARISTOTLE

THE INVISIBLE HAND: GOD'S INFLUENCE IN AMERICA'S HISTORY

Our founding fathers, and men like Yale President Ezra Stiles, seemed to sense the destiny of the young American nation.

George Washington, John Adams, Benjamin Franklin and Abraham Lincoln, to name only a few figures in American history, seemed to see clearly the providence of God behind the events of their day. The nation did not unfold by accident or happenstance, they insisted, but by divine design.

The settlement of America, timed as it was in the wake of the Reformation, assured its Christian foundations.

Nor could our founding fathers account for the victory over England, against such extreme odds, apart from the seeming intervention of God at key moments in the Revolutionary War.

In a major address before the Assembly of Connecticut in 1783, Ezra Stiles, then president of Yale, reviewed these events and suggested why near disasters time and time again suddenly turned to victories:

"In our lowest and most dangerous state, in 1776 and 1777, we sustained ourselves against the British army of sixty thousands troops, commanded by...the ablest generals Britain could procure throughout Europe, with a naval force of twenty-two thousand seaman in above eighty British men-of-war."

"Who but a Washington, inspired by Heaven," asked Stiles, could have conceived the surprise move upon the enemy at Princeton—that Christmas eve when Washington and his army crossed the Delaware?

"Who but the Ruler of the winds," he asked, could have delayed British reinforcements by three months of contrary ocean winds at a critical point of the war?

Or what but "a providential miracle," he insisted, at the last minute detected the treacherous scheme of traitor Benedict Arnold, which would have delivered the American army, including George Washington himself, into the hands of the enemy?

On the French role in the Revolution he added, "It is God who so ordered the balancing interests of nations as to produce an irresistible motive in the European maritime powers to take our part...."

A Remarkable View of America's Future.

Then the president of Yale seemed to view the future with remarkable clarity, as if looking directly into the Twentieth Century:

"We shall have a communication with

Replica of the Susan Constant docked at Jamestown

Washington crossing Delaware

all nations in commerce, manners, and science, beyond anything heretofore known in the world...

"...The English language...will probably become the vernacular tongue of more numerous millions than ever yet spake one language on earth."

"Navigation will carry the American flag around the globe itself...."

From the Scriptures he saw today's modern high-speed travel between continents and the world's explosion of technology. Declared Stiles:

"That prophecy of Daniel is now literally fulfilling—'there shall be a universal travelling to and fro, and knowledge shall be increased' (See Dan. 12:4).

"This knowledge will be brought home and treasured up in America, and being here digested and carried to the highest perfection, may reblaze back from America to Europe, Asia and Africa, and illumine the world with truth and liberty...."

But even then Stiles warned that the entire American system, good as it was, would prosper only as "men, not merely nominal Christians (Christians in name only), make it work." In view of God's hand in the long string of events that had produced a new nation, with new freedoms, Stiles concluded, "The United States are under peculiar obligations to become a holy people unto the Lord our God."

New Beginnings.

Major Christian events lie not only behind the founding of America as a nation, but also behind many of its individual states. The charters of all fifty states, carry religious language and acknowledge their foundations in God.

Virginia.

The First Charter of Virginia, providing for the settlement of Jamestown, was written before the Puritan Pilgrims arrived in America. It is here we find America's beginnings.

Dated April 10, 1606, the charter reads:

"We, greatly commending, and graciously accepting of, their Desires for the Furtherance of so noble a Work, which may, by the Providence of Almighty God, hereafter tend to the Glory of His Divine Majesty, in propagating of Christian Religion to such People, as yet live in Darkness and miserable Ignorance of the true Knowledge and Worship of God, and may in time bring the Infidels and Savages, living in those Parts, to human Civility, and to a settled and quiet Government."

When the settlers who founded the Jamestown colony landed at Cape Henry in April of 1607, they erected a large wooden cross and held a prayer meeting. It was their first act in the new land they had come to settle.

Pennsylvania.

Quaker William Penn was given what is now Pennsylvania in lieu of a monetary inheritance due his father, Admiral William Penn, discoverer of Bermuda.

Instead of using the land selfishly, Penn writes:

"I do, therefore, desire the Lord's wisdom to guide me, and those that may be concerned with me, that we do the thing that is truely wise and just."

The King of England gave to Penn what later became one of the largest states in the northeast United States, with the right to govern. A year later, the Duke of York also gave Penn what is now Delaware.

Penn clearly saw all of this as a trust from God.

"I eyed the Lord in obtaining it," he wrote, "and more was I drawn inward to look to Him, and to owe it to His hand and power than to any other way. I have so obtained it, and desire to keep it that I may not be unworthy of His love." A man of lesser character might have squandered this huge piece of real estate to the detriment of generations to come. But not Penn. He perceived that the God who had "given it to me through many difficulties, will, I believe, bless and make it the seed of a nation."

As a Quaker who had experienced persecution, he saw the colony as a land of religious freedom. So he wrote advertisements for his colony, printed them in six languages, and sent them to Europe.

Into Pennsylvania poured the Dutch, the Swedes, the Welsh, English Quakers, German groups, and, last of all, the Scots-Irish—all people under religious or economic oppression.

Pennsylvania did, in fact, become "the seed of a nation."

Washington.

In the Pacific Northwest, the names of missionaries Marcus and Narcissa Whitman stand next to Lewis and Clark.

Near Walla Walla in southeast Washington, the Whitman gravesites and a lonely, reconstructed mission (now a national historic site) vividly help recreate the story.

Medical doctor Marcus Whitman, an Easterner, first went west with the American Fur Company in 1835 to scout the territory. Against everyone's advice, he returned for his bride, convinced that "where wagons could go, women could go."

The seven-month journey proved extremely arduous. They had to contend with sick companions, frustrating delays, a slow-moving cattle herd, and an unwieldly wagon. Marcus left his wagon—reduced to a two wheeled cart—at Fort Boise before crossing the Blue Mountains, where he could follow only the trails of Indians and trappers.

Through all of this Narcissa maintained a deep and abiding faith in the Lord, revealed years later in a diary she had kept on the trek. Along with another missionary wife, Eliza Spaulding, she became the first white woman to cross the Rockies.

The Whitmans arrived safely in 1836 and opened a mission among the Cayuse at their landmark outpost on the Oregon trail, where they served for nine years.

On November 29, 1847, a band of Indians attacked the mission and killed Marcus Whitman, his wife, and nearly a dozen others. A few survivors escaped, and fifty were taken captive.

News of the tragedy sped to Congress in Washington, D.C., along with petitions from the settlers that the U.S. promptly establish territorial rule in the tense Northwest wilderness. Congress acted, and the Oregon territory emerged.

The Whitman's spiritual dedication left an example to the nation, and Narcissa left Americans a volume of richly detailed letters, read by thousands of schoolchildren, that offer an authentic glimpse into pioneer life.

WHEN AMERICA MOVED WEST

*The American Sunday School Union, the circuit riders,
even explorers built spiritual vigor into the fabric of
the American republic as its people pushed back the frontier.*

Some elements of today's society seem "deathly scared" of anything religious. They seem totally ignorant that Christians have given America the very moral fabric upon which the nation has prospered. The Bible has never threatened America. It has helped to build it.

The American Sunday School Movement: Planting Churches in a Fertile Land.

Perhaps no movement in early America undergirded its evangelism with the spirit of patriotism as did the American Sunday School Union.

The Sunday school movement had originated in England with Robert Raikes. It was transplanted to America by another Englishman, Robert May. It took root with special vigor around Philadelphia, and out of that city in 1824 came a national movement called the American Sunday School Union.

In the next century and a half it planted thousands of Sunday schools across America, following the migration west from the Appalachian cabins to the frontier towns and the isolated hovels of the western Indian. Churches eventually sprang up from the majority of these Sunday schools—more than three thousand of them in this century alone.

The American Sunday School Union's link to great past patriots is easy to document.

Its prime mover was Dr. Benjamin Rush, signer of the Declaration of Independence and the most eminent

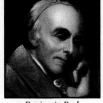
Benjamin Rush

American physician of his generation.

Among its original vice presidents was Bushrod Washington, nephew of George Washington. The American Sunday School Union originated probably the most widely circulated book ever written on George Washington.

Also among its early officers was John Marshall, one of the great Chief Justices of the United States Supreme Court.

Another long-time vice president was Pennsylvania Governor John Pollock who, as director of the United States Mint in Philadelphia, first inscribed on our coins the motto, "In God We Trust."

But one of the movements most illustrious figures, who served as a manager and vice president from the time of the American Sunday School Union's inception until his death eighteen years later, once found himself held captive aboard a British ship outside the city of Baltimore, near Fort McHenry. He watched "the rockets' red glare, the bombs bursting in air." Then Francis Scott Key wrote *The Star Spangled Banner*!

Circuit Riders: Evangelizing the Pioneers.

These were preachers on horseback, who roamed the wilderness in all kinds of weather to search out pioneers who needed to hear the gospel and Christians who needed encouragement. Though people were hidden in the wilderness, they missed few cabins.

Methodists took the initiative with the circuit rider concept. Probably the most amazing of them all was Francis Asbury. In the early 1800s, when thousands of pioneers left their homes and churches in the East and trekked through the Cumberland Gap into the forest beyond, Asbury went after them. He was determined to bring Jesus to them where they were.

Despite the peril of Indian attacks, the cold winters and the absence of roads, Asbury roamed the American wilderness for forty years. He planted the seeds of the gospel everywhere, like a spiritual Johnny Appleseed, and then came back year after year to examine the harvest.

It is said that Francis Asbury may have traveled more than one quarter million

miles. And he preached some twenty-five thousand sermons!

Before the Revolutionary War, the Anglican church and the Congregationalists had dominated American Protestantism. But they weren't prepared for the great migration West. The Anglicans, in particular, were content to remain entrenched in their churches along the Eastern seaboard. The Methodists, still rather obscure on the American religious scene, sent out circuit riders. The Baptists sent their "farmer-preachers." A half century later, these two groups had surged far ahead. Those churches that had once dominated America's religious scene were now far outdistanced by these who had dared to leave the comfort of their own churches and evangelize.

The early frontier circuit rider, and others of like spirit, knew that in order to spread the gospel far and wide, they had to go where the people were.

The Bible Has Never Threatened America. It Has Helped to Build It.

Christian Explorers: Blazing a Trail for God and Country.

John Wesley Powell, the famous American explorer who discovered the Colorado River, once studied at what is now Wheaton College in Illinois and also at Oberlin College in Ohio, founded by evangelist Charles Finney. Powell, son of a circuit-riding preacher, taught science at a Christian school before leaving to explore the West.

In 1859 Powell, who had one arm amputated during the Civil War, put together an 11-man expedition to

John Wesley Powell

explore the rapids of the Colorado River and the Grand Canyon where no white man had ventured before. Among the expedition's daring task-force of geologists, historians, and various scientists were three ministers.

Some of the men later turned back. Indians killed three members of the expedition. Yet those who completed the trip told the world of an unimaginable frontier wilderness and beauty.

What made Powell push on when he might have fled in fear? One biographer put it this way: "He was made by wandering, by hard labor, and by the Bible...."

In 1826 Jedediah Smith, Bible-totin' trailblazer and American explorer, became the first white man to cross the Great Salt Lake Desert and the Sierra Nevada Mountains. His daring took him as far as Fort Vancouver in the Pacific Northwest. Jedediah Smith was killed by Comanche Indians near the Cimarron River in southwestern Kansas on May 27, 1831.

Christian Colleges: Educating a New Generation.

Evangelical Christians of an earlier year planted many of America's colleges as the nation moved west, including such major institutions today as Northwestern University near Chicago (founded by the Methodists) and the University of California at Berkeley (founded by evangelical Presbyterians).

Those who today would secularize America destroy the nation's very heritage.

THE AWAKENING OF AMERICA

Two great spiritual awakenings in the land—one before the Revolution, the other after it—may have saved our young nation from calamity in its most formative years.

President Calvin Coolidge once said, "America was born in a revival of religion."

The preaching of Jonathan Edwards and George Whitefield changed the spiritual landscape of America before the Revolution. As catalysts for what became known as the "First Great Awakening," they may well have also helped set in motion some of the very forces that eventually brought America its political freedoms.

Jonathan Edwards: Brilliant of Mind and Spirit.

Most historians agree that Jonathan Edwards stands with Benjamin Franklin as "one of the two outstanding minds in the America of the eighteenth century."

Edwards entered Yale at thirteen and graduated valedictorian at seventeen. As he grew in his Christian faith at Yale, he became somewhat of a "mystic," in the better sense, in his quest to know more of God. Said Edwards following his conversion:

"God's excellency, his wisdom, his purity and love, seemed to appear in everything; in the sun, moon and stars; in the clouds, and blue sky; in the grass, flowers, trees; in the water, and all

nature; which used greatly to fix my mind."

Edwards fell in love with a prominent young Christian lady, Sarah Pierrepont, who was noted for her charm, her flashing wit and a joyous repartee. She proved the ideal pastor's wife for Edwards, who took over his father-in-law's prestigious pulpit in North-hampton, Massachusetts, two years after their marriage. Jonathan and Sarah Edwards eventually raised a remarkably fine family of eleven children.

Edwards came to Northhampton at a time when spirituality was at a low ebb. The conditions he describes among the young people might sound much like conditions of today:

"Licentiousness for some years greatly prevailed among the youth of the town: there were many of them very much addicted to night walking and frequenting the tavern, and lewd practices wherein some by their example exceedingly corrupted others."

Then revival began in 1734, while Jonathan Edwards was preaching a series of sermons on justification by faith

Jonathan Edwards

alone. Conversions began, first the young then their elders. A notorious young woman was saved. It was like a "flash of lightning" to the young people. There were those who agonized, and those who rejoiced. Wrote Edwards:

"...in the spring and summer following, anno 1735, the town seemed to be full of the presence of God; it never was so full of love, nor of joy, and yet so full of distress, as it was then."

By 1736 Edward's church had 300 new converts, and news of the revival had spread throughout New England.

George Whitefield: The Voice Heard by Thousands.

It took a new surge when George Whitefield arrived from England in 1740 for two years of evangelism in America.

George Whitefield

Whitefield had already risen to prominence as a key figure in the Wesleyan revivals underway in England—a great movement of God there triggered by a group of Christian students at Oxford University.

In those days evangelists did not enjoy the advantage of microphones, but Whitefield didn't need one. At Bristol, England, he had preached to 20,000 at one gathering and all could hear. In America he preached to five thousand on the Boston Commons and eight thousand at once in the fields.

"Sinners in the Hands of an Angry God."

In New England the revival reached its peak in 1741, and it was in July at Enfield, Massachusetts, that Edwards preached his most famous sermon, "Sinners in the Hands of an Angry God."

Some modern critics have passed this off as the "religious fanaticism" of an earlier era. Yet Edwards did not deliver this sermon in what some might describe as "hellfire and brimstone" style. It is said that he did not raise his voice nor even move his arms, though his typically good diction and enunciation made every word ring clear. As he hammered home the judgment of God, point upon point, each listener felt the impact of his own guilt.

Was this really the same Jonathan Edwards who spoke so frequently on the love, and grace and beauty, and majesty of God?

Yes, because Edwards became convinced that one could not really understand the great love of God until he also understood the awfulness of sin.

There was such conviction of sin that day that Edwards had to wait some time until the congregation quieted down. He finally prayed, descended from the pulpit and discoursed with the people. They closed with a hymn and dismissed.

During little more that two years, from 1740 to 1742, some 25,000 to 50,000 people were added to the New England churches, out of a total population of only 300,000. The movement changed the entire moral tone of New England for the better and justly earned the name of a "Great Awakening."

Spreading Fire: Awakening in the Middle Colonies.

It fell to others to spread the revival from New England into New Jersey, Pennsylvania and the middle colonies. God chose men like Gilbert Tennant, whose father, a Presbyterian minister in remote Neshaminy, Bucks County, Pennsylvania, singlehandedly schooled Gilbert in his own home to be a minister. He built a log cabin in his yard to use as a school, where he taught Gilbert, his younger sons—and fifteen others—the languages, logic, theology. He also imparted to them an evangelical passion which sent them out flaming evangelists.

Gilbert Tennant, his brothers and their handful of dedicated young associates saw conversions wherever they preached, and revival began to spread throughout the middle colonies.

Some of the clergy looked down their noses at William Tennant's "Log College" and branded his graduates "half educated enthusiasts." But Tennant may have had the last laugh. Two of them eventually became presidents of Princeton!

Revival Reaches the South.

Meanwhile, the revival spread into Virginia and the southern colonies—in three stages.

Samuel Davies, one of the "Log College" graduates and later president of the College of New Jersey (Princeton), planted the first phase. The preaching of Baptist Shubal Stearns and his brother-in-law, Daniel Marshall, both products of the New England awakening, spread the revival, like wildfire into Virginia and North Carolina.

Devereuz Jarrat, an evangelical Anglican turned Methodist in spirit, fanned the revival's third phase in the southern colonies. Suddenly Methodists, like the Baptists, sprang up everywhere. Circuit riders spread the Good News, and Virginia-North Carolina became the cradle of Methodism.

The Second Great Awakening.

Such movements of God were not to be the last in the history of early America. By the close of the 1700's, the nation it seemed was headed again for disaster. Thousands of colonial Americans, until then clustered mostly along the Eastern seaboard, began to pull up roots and head West through the Cumberland Gap.

Conditions at that time did not exactly produce a territory of churchgoers. Once out into the frontier, many left their churches behind. Life became tough and rough. Morals declined.

One writer describes the scene aptly: "Corn liquor flowed freely... gun and rope settled far too many legal disputes. The West was crowded with thieves and murderers, with neither courts of law nor public opinion to raise a rebuke." Sexual sin abounded.

Christians who cared about the souls of men and the future of the country saw the peril. If such a spiritual drift should continue among the thousands of settlers already in the Alleghenies and beyond, it could bring down the judgment of God upon the entire young nation.

Yet only a thin system of trails and waterways connected the colonies with that vast wilderness beyond the mountains. Humanly speaking, it seemed impossible for godly men to change the course of events.

But God intervened in a mighty movement now known as the Second Great Awakening. The event surely

> # Thousands Were Swept into Churches ...More Than 10,000 in Kentucky Alone Between 1800 and 1803.

helped reverse the spiritual skid and saved America from calamity.

Where and when did the great western revival begin?

Birth of the Camp-Meetings.

Most historians pinpoint Kentucky's Logan County about 1799, when several Methodist and Presbyterian preachers joined efforts. Soon word of a mini-revival spread. Kentuckians came from miles around. The crowds grew, and soon visitors had to camp out for one, two or three nights. Men chopped down more trees to accommodate the crowds, and arranged split-log benches to create a church-in-the-wilderness.

A great meeting at Bourbon County's Cane Ridge in August, 1801, climaxed the fervor. It extended over several days and drew crowds estimated as high as 15,000, an incredible figure in view of the scanty population at that time.

One historian describes this vivid scene of an early camp meeting:

"The governor of our State was with us and encouraging the work. They are commonly collected in small circles of ten or twelve, closely adjoining another circle and all engaged in singing Watt's

and Hart's hymns; and then a minister steps upon a stump or log, and begins an exhortation or sermon, when as many as can hear collect around him."

Another describes the impressive scene at night: "The glare of campfires, ...earnest prayers,...sobs, shrieks, shouts."

It was a time that many families, and especially children, never forgot.

The high emotional pitch of the meetings triggered no small controversy, especially among staid clergy of the East. Despite admitted emotional excesses, the revival movement spread and had a profound effect in transforming the lives and morals of western society. Thousands were swept into churches—more than 10,000 in Kentucky alone between 1800 and 1803.

The revival and its impact eventually spread beyond the Kentucky borders, but camp meetings took on more dignity. They became well organized, and the camp meeting established itself as a legitimate Protestant innovation that helped bring the gospel to the masses. Its format, in fact, laid the foundations for the later campaigns of mass evangelism that still typify 20th century evangelicalism.

Typical Camp Meeting Scene

WITHOUT MICROPHONE OR TELEVISION

In the Nineteenth Century two great evangelists—Charles Finney and Dwight L. Moody—arose to bring America back on spiritual course. A ballplayer who could run the bases in fourteen seconds followed them.

Like the children of Israel, Americans have been prone to forget their spiritual heritage. In Israel's case, God sent prophets to forestall judgment In the nineteenth century and the early part of this century, God sent to the American scene:

A lawyer

A shoe salesman

And a major league ballplayer.

Charles G. Finney: From Law to Grace.

In 1830 lawyer Charles G. Finney preached for six months at Rochester, New York, and saw one hundred thousand souls make a profession of faith in Jesus Christ. It is estimated that the preaching of Finney, who founded Oberlin College in Ohio and served as its first president, influenced change in one half million lives.

Finney did not inherit his religious bent. In his home he never heard the name of God, except in blasphemy. Though reared in the backwoods of New York state, he emerged to study law and pursue in Adams, New York, what promised to be a brilliant legal career.

Since Finney's law books contained many references to the Bible, he bought one for reference. But he always made sure it was hid under other volumes when anyone else was around.

Finney visited the Presbyterian church in town and found the congregation praying for revival. The young lawyer offered only scorn and ridicule until young people in the church, led by the girl Finney would eventually marry, began to pray for him. The Spirit began to convict of sin. Finney could not eat or sleep. Finally one evening he fled to the woods on the edge of town, poured out his sins to God and found great release.

He raced back into town to shout out the news of his salvation—in offices, in homes, on the street. Within twenty-four hours he had won twenty-four to the Lord, among them another lawyer and a distiller!

Finney dropped law and began to plead the cause of Jesus Christ. He launched into evangelism and took onto his team a man named Nash, who made prayer his sole and all-consuming role. When Finney preached, Nash stayed behind and prayed. Wherever Finney conducted campaigns—in

London, New York, or elsewhere—thousands responded. In Boston, fifty thousand accepted the Lord in just one week.

When Finney preached in Philadelphia, "a number of lumberjacks who had floated their logs down the river took in the meeting. Many were converted, and on returning to their work eighty miles upstream, they took the story of salvation with them. At home they organized prayer circles, held family devotions, conducted simple services. On returning within a year's time they asked for a minister. Five thousand, the lumbermen reported, had turned to the Lord in their region—and they were without a preacher!"

"What will you do with Jesus Christ?" Finney always demanded a verdict on this all—important issue. Many of those converted went on to exert a profound social impact in their day. Finney continued as educator and evangelist until his death in 1875.

Dwight L Moody: From Selling Shoes to Saving Souls.

Chicago can never erase the memory of the great disaster that befell her little more than one hundred years ago. On an October Sunday evening in 1871, ominous flames erupted on the city's south side. By midnight the entire populace was fleeing in panic as the inferno swept northward block by block, reducing the city to ashes.

The great Chicago fire destroyed both the home and the church of an evangelist named Dwight L. Moody, along with the impressive Chicago YMCA, which he had founded. But in Moody's eyes it was not the worst catastrophe that could happen to man. Far worse that anyone should not hear clearly the gospel. Moody quickly rebuilt his church and pressed forward.

By the time of the Chicago fire, Moody had already uplifted Jesus Christ to millions at home and abroad, but by the time of his death more than a quarter century later some would estimate his total audience in the tens of millions.

Moody's spiritual life started in the back of a shoe store in Boston in 1855 when a dry-goods salesman led Moody to Jesus Christ. Moody soon went west to Chicago and established himself as a first-rate shoe salesman. Moody also began rounding up street urchins from the poor section of Chicago's north side and before long his burgeoning mission Sunday school hosted hundreds weekly. In 1860 even President-elect Abraham Lincoln dropped in on Moody's class.

In 1873 the rising Moody, with his songleader Ira Sankey, launched a campaign in the British Isles. Things started slowly, but they picked up momentum. Crowds grew. The campaign extended into weeks, then months—first Edinburgh, later Glasgow, finally London. Thousands were converted, homes were transformed, lives changed—genuinely, permanently—an impact that would be felt throughout England

"What Will You Do With Jesus Christ?"

Charles Finney

for decades. When the campaign closed two years later, all Great Britain was talking about Moody and Sankey. He later returned for two more highly successful campaigns.

Moody's preaching mission at England's erudite Cambridge University touched off a spiritual revival that ultimately sent hundreds of students around the world as missionaries.

But back home, America, too, needed Moody's message, perhaps as never before. The Civil War, like all wars, had disrupted general morality. People chased after easy wealth. Corruption penetrated high political office.

Before launching a campaign in Philadelphia, Moody touched off a small revival at Princeton University. At Philadelphia one evening President Ulysses S. Grant and several of his Cabinet sat on the platform. There was the New York campaign of 1876—and many more to follow in the cities and towns across America, spanning at least a quarter century until his death during a Kansas City campaign in 1899, just a few days before the turn of the Twentieth Century.

Billy Sunday: From the Basepath to the "Sawdust Trail."

Flash now to the early twentieth century and the impact of a one-time major league ball player named Billy Sunday, who played with the then Chicago White Stockings.

Fans labeled him the only man who could round the diamond touching every base in fourteen seconds.

Billy Sunday received Christ at the Pacific Garden Mission in Chicago around the time Dwight L. Moody founded his Bible Institute two miles away.

Sunday continued in pro ball four more years, until resigning for full-time evangelism. His great physical stamina as a ball player carried over well into his new career, during which he would preach twenty thousand times! In 1917, in New York, a million and a half people heard Sunday during a ten-week campaign. Some two million, it is said, gave their hearts to God during the Sunday campaigns, which spanned a quarter of a century.

Sunday would roll up his sleeves and deliver his sermons machine-gun style, roaming vigorously about the platform. No one denied his color and showman-
Billy Sunday

ship, but there was much more—the historic gospel that transformed the lives of millions.

Three men out of the nineteenth century helped set great spiritual forces in motion. There were millions across America whose lives, homes, and careers were salvaged, redirected, transformed, as a direct result.

Had not God singled out a handful of individuals in each century who could help reverse the inevitable degeneracy in the hearts of men, America by now might have died as a major nation.

POTENT ANSWERS TO PERSISTENT PRAYER

BY J. EDWIN ORR

In New York's Manhattan in 1857 thousands attended noon meetings, reported newspaper editor Horace Greeley. In Portland, Oregon, a half century later, department stores closed for prayer.

Spiritual conditions in the United States deteriorated in the middle of the 19th century. People were making money "hand over fist," and when they did, they turned their backs on God.

But a man of prayer, Jeremiah Lanphier, started a prayer meeting in the upper room of the Consistory Building of the Dutch Reformed Church in Manhattan. He advertised it. Only six people (from a population of one million) showed up.

But the following week there were 14, and then 23. They decided to meet every day. Soon they filled the Dutch Reformed Church, the Methodist Church on John Street, then every public building in downtown New York.

Famed newspaper editor Horace Greeley sent a reporter with horse and buggy riding around the prayer meetings to see how many men were praying. In one hour, he could only get to 12 meetings, but he counted 6,100 men. Then a landslide of prayer began.

People began to be converted (10,000 a week) in New York City. The movement spread throughout New England. Church bells would bring people to prayer at eight in the morning, twelve noon, and six in the evening. The revival went up the Hudson and down the Mohawk. Baptists had so many people to baptize, they couldn't get them into their churches. They went down to the river, cut a big square in the ice, and baptized them in cold water.

In one year, more than one million people were converted. The revival crossed the Atlantic, broke out in Northern Ireland and Scotland and Wales and England, South Africa, South India— anywhere there was an evangelical cause, there was revival—and its effect was felt for 40 years. It began in a movement of prayer...it was sustained by a movement of prayer.

The 1905 Revival: The Shaking of a Nation.

That movement lasted a generation, but at the turn of the 20th century there was need of awakening again. There were special prayer meetings at Moody Bible Institute, at the Keswick Convention in New England, in Melbourne, in the Mildrey Hills of India, at Won San in

THE REBIRTH OF AMERICA

Korea...all around the world people were praying that there might be another great awakening in the 20th century. God did indeed answer these prayers—in 1905.

Let me give you two examples: first, the student world. One of the leaders of the revival of 1905 was a young man of the Ivy League who later became perhaps the world's most famous professor of world missions. When he was at Yale in 1905, 25% of the student body was enrolled in prayer meetings and Bible studies!

The ministers of Atlantic City reported that of a population of 50,000 in that city, they knew of only 50 adults who were unconverted. In Portland, Oregon, two hundred and forty department stores closed from 11 to 2 for prayer and signed an agreement among themselves so that no one would cheat and stay open. That's what was happening in the United States in 1905.

That revival of 1905 in the United States was linked to the famous Welsh revival of 1904, which swept like a tidal wave over Wales—where 100,000 people were converted in a five-month period. Five years later, J.P. Morgan wrote a book to debunk the revival. His main criticism was that of the 100,000 that joined churches in the five months of the revival, after five years, only 80,000 still stood. Only 80,000!

The social impact of the Wales revival was astounding. Judges were presented with white gloves: they had no cases to try. No rapes, no robberies, no murders, no burglaries, no embezzlements, nothing. The District Consuls held emergency meetings to discuss what to do with the police, now that they were unemployed.

Drunkenness was cut in half. The illegitimate birth rate dropped 44 percent in two counties within a year of the beginning of the revival, so great was its impact.

❦

Revival—the inrush of the Spirit into the body that threatens to become a corpse.

D.M. PANTON

Entire city pauses for prayer even at the high tide of business.

Remarkable outburst of gospel sentiment… noonday meetings draw congregations unprecedented in numbers.

For two hours at midday all Denver was held in a spell…. The marts of trade were deserted between noon and two o'clock this afternoon, and all worldly affairs were forgotten, and the entire city was given over to meditation of higher things. The Spirit of the Almighty pervaded every nook. Going to and coming from the great meetings, the thousands of men and women radiated this Spirit which filled them, and the clear Colorado sunshine was made brighter by the reflected glow of the light of God shining from happy faces. Seldom has such a remarkable sight been witnessed—an entire great city, in the middle of a busy weekday, bowing before the throne of heaven and asking and receiving the blessing of the King of the Universe.

DENVER POST/JANUARY 20, 1905

THE SYMBOLS OF A NATION'S FAITH

"In no other place in the United States are there so many, and such varied official evidences of deep and abiding faith in God on the part of Governments as there are in Washington." —Senator Robert Byrd.

June 25, 1962. The Supreme Court had just declared prayer in the schools unconstitutional. Senator Robert Byrd of West Virginia, a Bible teacher and respected member of the U.S. Legislature, was so moved by the disastrous decision that two days later he delivered an address to his colleagues in Congress reminding them of the Christian symbolism throughout their own city.

He verbally escorted them to the Library of Congress, the Washington Monument, the Lincoln Memorial, the Jefferson Memorial, the Supreme Court, and other landmarks. Then he concluded:

"Inasmuch as our greatest leaders have shown no doubt about God's proper place in the American birthright, can we, in our day, dare do less?"

A sampling of these follow:

Prayer window, U.S. Capitol

The Capitol.

Every session of the House and the Senate begins with prayer. Each house has its own chaplain.

The Eighty-third Congress set aside a small room in the Capitol, just off the rotunda, for the private prayer and meditation of members of Congress. The room is always open when Congress is in session, but it is not open to the public. The room's focal point is a stained glass window showing George Washington kneeling in prayer. Behind him is etched these words from Psalm 16:1: "Preserve me, O God, for in Thee do I put my trust."

Inside the rotunda is a picture of the Pilgrims about to embark from Holland on the sister ship of the *Mayflower*, the *Speedwell*. The ship's revered chaplain, Brewster, who later joined the *Mayflower*, has open on his lap the Bible. Very clear are the words, "the New Testament according to our Lord and Savior, Jesus Christ." On the sail is the motto of the Pilgrims, "In God We Trust, God With Us."

The phrase, "In God We Trust," appears opposite the President of the Senate, who is the Vice President of the United States. The same phrase, in large words inscribed in the marble, backdrops the Speaker of the House of Representatives.

The Jefferson Memorial

The Supreme Court.

Above the head of the Chief Justice of the Supreme Court are the Ten Commandments, with the great American eagle protecting them. Moses is included among the great lawgivers in Herman A. MacNeil's marble sculpture group on the east front. The crier who opens each session closes with the words, "God save the United States and the Honorable Court."

The Washington Monument.

Engraved on the metal cap on the top of the Washington Monument are the words: "Praise be to God." Lining the walls of the stairwell are such biblical phrases as "Search the Scriptures," "Holiness to the Lord," "Train up a child in the way he should go, and when he is old he will not depart from it."

The Library Of Congress.

Numerous quotations from Scripture can be found within its walls. One reminds each American of his responsibility to his Maker: "What doth the Lord require of thee, but to do justly and love mercy and walk humbly with thy God" (Micah 6:8)

Another in the lawmaker's library preserves the Psalmist's acknowledgment that all nature reflects the order and beauty of the Creator. "The heavens declare the glory of God, and the firmament showeth His handiwork" (Psalm 19:1).

And still another reference: "The light shineth in darkness, and the darkness comprehendeth it not" (John 1:5).

Lincoln Memorial.

Millions have stood in the Lincoln Memorial and gazed up at the statue of the great Abraham Lincoln. The sculptor

who chiseled the features of Lincoln in granite all but seems to make Lincoln speak his own words inscribed into the walls.

"...That this Nation, under God, shall have a new birth of freedom, and that government of the people, by the people, for the people, shall not perish from the earth."

At the opposite end, on the north wall, his Second Inaugural Address alludes to "God," the "Bible," "providence," "the Almighty," and "divine attributes."

It then continues:

"As was said 3000 years ago, so it still must be said, 'The judgments of the Lord are true and righteous altogether.'"

Jefferson Memorial.

On the south banks of Washington's Tidal Basin, Thomas Jefferson still speaks:

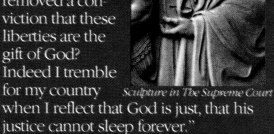

Sculpture in The Supreme Court

"God who gave us life gave us liberty. Can the liberties of a nation be secure when we have removed a conviction that these liberties are the gift of God? Indeed I tremble for my country when I reflect that God is just, that his justice cannot sleep forever."

Senator Byrd cites these words of Jefferson as "a forceful and explicit warning that to remove God from this country will destroy it."

Bronze Plaque in Dirksen Office Building

A NATION ESTABLISHED:
A Conclusion.

In his stirring anthem to the solidity of the Christian faith, George Chapman penned the now-familiar words, "How firm a foundation, ye saints of the Lord, is laid for your faith in His excellent Word!" And how appropriate are these words when correlated to America's glorious heritage.

This nation, without reasonable doubt, was established on the firm foundation of Scripture. Our forefathers, brilliant as they were, openly acknowledged the true genius behind the new system to be the eternal principles of God's Word. The most fundamental concepts of the republic find their roots in the Bible. From the beginning, the basis for law and government in American society was decidedly biblical. What's more, the new land was forged through the energy of the Judeo-Christian work ethic.

The United States in her first century of existence knew the stinging reality of conflict. There were wars, assassinations, injustices, catastrophes, and plagues of disease. But the young nation endured, for its moral fabric had been woven with the durable threads of Scriptural truth. Societal ills, like slavery, were ultimately recognized for what they were: violations of God's standard.

The record of the establishment of America bears the clear stamp of Christian influence. The impact of the Gospel is evident in the leaders chosen, the laws written, and the sweeping changes brought about through the transforming power of Christ in individual lives and corporate experience. America was not formed a nation apart from God, but a nation under God.

AMERICA TODAY:

A NATION
ADRIFT

IS THE GREAT AMERICAN DREAM TURNING INTO A NIGHTMARE?

America has rejected God in dealing with the issues of life.

God has showered upon America 200 years of blessing. As she acknowledged and obeyed her Creator, God elevated her from infancy to a place of world leadership. He has allowed her to enjoy unprecedented wealth, freedom and influence.

America has led the world in medical and technological advancement. The nation has pioneered in space, pushed back the frontiers of science, and given its citizens the world's highest standard of living.

America has opened her arms to millions of immigrants and refugees, first from Europe, then more recently from the Far East: Laotians, boat people, Vietnamese. Add to this the stream of new residents from Mexico and other Latin countries.

While other nations build barbed-wire fences to keep people from getting out, America greets a long line of people waiting to get in.

With grateful and humble hearts, Americans once honored the God who granted her blessings and freedoms. But slowly—almost imperceptibly—she began to attribute her blessings not so much to God, but to man.

A Fatal Lapse of Memory.

Forgetting to acknowledge "the Power that hath made and preserved us a nation," her citizens began to congratulate themselves on their own achievements—to celebrate man, while relegating God to the back seat. The god of secular humanism began to infiltrate all of her institutions.

Wallowing in materialism, self-centeredness and pride, many Americans decided that they really did not need God after all. Some began to tamper with God's absolute standards, and to tolerate what they would never have allowed before—in their own lives or in society around them. That which God says is *never* right could be *sometimes* right, depending on the situation. Courts that had once legislated against immorality began to grant freedom to every man to "do that which was right in his own eyes" (see Judges 17:6 and 21:5). Lines of right and wrong blurred. In time, all sorts of ungodly behavior became acceptable—even admired. Americans no longer were shocked. Eyes grew "accustomed to the dark." Few citizens rose up in outrage.

When God fades from a nation's

75

conscience, one can justify almost anything.

New American Meanings for Old Words

God says, "Thou shalt not kill." Americans gave murder a new name and indifferently aborted 1,374,000 unborn babies last year (1984) alone.

Many tried to camouflage sin with new terminology.

God calls it "drunkenness." We call it "alcoholism—a social disease."

God calls it "sodomy." We call it "homosexuality—gay rights, an alternate lifestyle."

God calls it "perversion." We call it "pornography—adult entertainment."

God calls it "immorality." We call it the "new morality."

God calls it "cheating." We call it "abnormal social development."

With the dissolving of absolutes, America's crime rate has spiraled, until it now costs taxpayers $2 billion a year. A serious crime is committed every 3.5 seconds, one robbery every 83 seconds, one murder every 27 minutes.

Drug addiction and alcoholism are in pandemic proportions. More than 500,000 heroin addicts live in the United States, and 43 million Americans have experimented with marijuana.

The United States now has more than 9 million alcoholics.

Suicide is the second largest killer of teenagers.

Teenage pregnancies, incest and sexual child abuse draw national attention. More than 2 million Americans a year contract gonorrhea.

Pornographic magazines (more than 20 million a year) and books crowd the newsstands. Video-cassette stores now market the products of X-rated theatres. One out of every two marriages ends in divorce. Some 1.3 million unmarried couples now live together, according to the United States Census Bureau. The IRS has made abortion clinics "charitable" organizations, therefore exempt from taxes.

America once legislated against those things that God said to be wrong. But gradually we began to tolerate, then accept, then condone openly, and even promote, that which was once unthinkable. The perversion and degradation that once made us blush are now flaunted before the eyes of a nation that was conceived in the fear of God. It has happened, little by little, right before our eyes—not because someone forced it on us, but seemingly because we did not care. We just didn't care.

And so, we are living out the truth of God's Word given to a past generation:

"And it shall be, when the Lord thy God shall have brought thee into the land which He swore unto thy fathers, to give thee great and goodly cities, which thou buildest not, and houses full of all good things, which thou filledst not, and wells digged, which thou diggedst not, vineyard and olive trees, which thou plantedst not, when thou shalt have eaten and be full; then beware lest thou forget the Lord . . . and thou say in thine heart, My power and the might of mine hand hath gotten me this wealth" (Deut. 6:10-12; 8:17).

WE CAN SEE THESE SYMPTOMS OF MATERIALISM THROUGHOUT OUR SOCIETY, BUT THE MOST VISIBLE ONE IS LOSS OF COURAGE. PEOPLE STAND BY AND WATCH A FELLOW CITIZEN BEING BEATEN OR STABBED AND THEY DO NOT INTERFERE. THEY ARE AFRAID. OUR POLITICAL LEADERS WATCH COMMUNISM GOBBLE UP OTHER NATIONS AND THEY DO NOTHING. THEY ARE AFRAID. PEOPLE COMPLAIN IN PRIVATE ABOUT THE STATE OF AFFAIRS BUT WILL NOT SPEAK OUT IN PUBLIC. THEY ARE AFRAID...

GENERAL LEWIS W. WALT

A NATION ADRIFT

BY SENATOR JESSE HELMS

In the brief history of our own country since we gained our independence, we can look back upon a tremendous heritage of political freedom founded upon a biblical faith and a biblical understanding of the nature of man. Moreover, we can look back upon the material signs of God's blessing in a fruitful and bounteous country, with success in almost every enterprise in war and peace.

American Institutions: Under Attack.

But within my own lifetime, I have seen the most ferocious assaults on Christian faith and morals; first on the part of the intellectual community, and then on the part of the government. Especially in the last 25 years, the federal government has not even tried to conceal its hostility to religion; now, with many of our churches in disarray, the attack is being prepared against the family as the last bastion opposing the totalitarian state. Militant atheists and socialists have gone very far in imposing their view of life and man on almost every American institution.

And what have we reaped as a nation from our many personal and collective delinquencies? Atheistic schools, rampaging crimes, God-forsaken homes, drugs, abortion, pornography, permissiveness, a sense of cynicism, and spiritual desolation absolutely unprecedented in our country's history.

The Israelites in their time also opted for the "New Morality." They were as enthusiastic as many of our contemporary thinkers about situation ethics, for we read, "In those days, there was no king in Israel; but every man did what was right in his own eyes" (Judges 17:6).

When Did the Drift Begin?

It is debatable at just what point the United States began to drift away from its Christian heritage. But I think we reached that point when many Americans turned away from the idea of salvation through Christ to that of salvation through technology or science or material affluence or the welfare state.

When all these turned out to be dead ends, Americans began to seek escape, and the purveyors of drugs and pornography and vicarious violence were there to meet the need. Human nature left to its own devices has always been a wretched failure at explaining the meaning and destiny of life.

America's Only Hope.

I have often meditated upon why God chose the time and place He did for his Son to be born into the world. In the long preparation for the coming of Christ, the world had seen the tremendous achievements of many civilizations. But neither the intellectual brilliance of the Greeks; or the sober morals of the ancient Romans; nor the technological and organizational genius of the later Romans were enough to still the discontent of human hearts. God chose an obscure outpost of a decadent empire as the birthplace of His Son,

and upon all the debris of human pride and presumption there came forth the anointed Saviour. From that day to this, there has been only one Light of the World, one Hope of Mankind.

All through His earthly life, this Person took pains to point out that He was not in any way a political messiah. Quite the reverse holds true in Washington today, where many politicians and many factions contend relentlessly for the honor of being the very political messiah who will solve all our problems if only we give them more money and more power.

Our People Look in the Wrong Direction for Their Deliverance.

Looking the Right Direction, Learning the Right Lessons.

By and large, our people look in the wrong direction for their deliverance. As Christians we need to work with missionary zeal to reinstate the rule of Christ in our sadly demoralized country.

As the Israelites learned time and again from the last of their enemies, it was only by repentance and submission to the God of their Fathers that they could survive and prosper.

I pray every day for a rebirth of the spiritual values that made us a nation in the first place. If the Spirit of God were to rouse 200 million Americans to action, there is no describing the greatness and glory in store for this country, or the blessings forthcoming to nations now held captive if and when, once again, the United States rededicates itself to the cause of freedom under God's Law.

79

THE MYTHS THAT COULD DESTROY AMERICA

*It is a dangerous thing when we too easily accept
new ideas as truth.*

BY ERWIN LUTZER

MYTH NUMBER ONE

"The Battle Isn't Real."

A news reporter asked a pedestrian, " Do you know what the two greatest problems in America are?"

"I don't know and I don't care!" the man responded.

"Then you've got both of them!" was the abrupt reply.

Although our nation is rotting on the inside and hostile forces are determined to take away our freedom, our greatest problem might just be that there are too many people who neither know nor care.

Not until all is lost will many awake to the painful reality that America as we once knew it is gone.

As humanism moves society farther away from Christian values, it will become increasingly intolerant of competing viewpoints. In a smear campaign aimed at what Norman Lear calls "the new right," Christians have been painted in the same hues as the Nazis and the Ku Klux Klan. Because Christians believe in the freedoms that America has enjoyed for 200 years, they are considered the lunatic fringe. Make no mistake about the intention of these secularists: It is to discredit the voice of Christians so that America will tolerate only *one* view. The battle lines are between two religions: Humanism vs. Judeo-Christian beliefs. Clearly two world-views are on a collision course.

History documents the final results of an intolerant humanistic state. According to some estimates, Chairman Mao of China is credited with the death of 30 million Chinese; Stalin 30-60 million Russians and Hitler 15 million people, of which 6 million were Jews.

These people died because the state believed that matter was the final reality, hence there is no God, no immorality, no final judgment. God was dethroned and the state was put in its place.

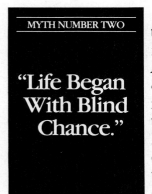

MYTH NUMBER TWO

"Life Began With Blind Chance."

Today the doctrine of evolution is in disarray. Although the man on the street may not know it yet, the theory of evolution is being dismantled through modern discoveries. Darwinism has fallen on hard times. Even the head of the French Academy of Science candidly admits, "Evolution is a fairy tale for adults."

But that is not what the public at large hears.

Clarence Darrow once argued in the 1925 Scopes Trial that it is "bigotry for public schools to teach only one theory of origins." Now that evolution is entrenched in public education, the American Civil Liberties Union, despite its own cries on behalf of pluralism, insists that only one theory of origins be taught. Bigotry has returned to the public classroom.

To settle for evolution or "the big bang" theory without God begs a thousand scientific questions. Where did the original energy and matter come from? What caused the explosion? How could impersonal forces acting randomly construct a universe whose planets rotate with such precision that we set our clocks by them? It is preposterous to believe that "nothing times nobody equals everything!"

On a television program, author Aldous Huxley once responded to the question of why evolution was so readily accepted. He admitted "the reason we accepted Darwinism even without proof is because we didn't want God to interfere with our sexual mores."

There you have it. The real reason modern man does not want to believe in God is he wants no interference from the Creator.

While many scientists secretly admit that evidence for the evolutionary fairy tale is crumbling, they refuse to run toward God. If one does not wish to find God, he will not—regardless of the evidence.

Yet if man is only a biological accident, the product of chance chemical reactions of impersonal forces, it is virtually impossible to make any distinction between right and wrong.

MYTH NUMBER THREE

"We Can Have Morality Without Religion."

On November 17, 1980, the Supreme Court struck down a Kentucky law that required the posting of the Ten Commandments in public school classrooms. The Court said that the Ten Commandments were "plainly religious"...and may induce children to read, meditate upon, perhaps to venerate and to obey the commandments."

Morality and religion can never be separated. In fact, the very basis of morality is the existence of God.

When the Supreme Court asked that the Ten Commandments be removed from Kentucky classrooms, they had no moral code to replace them. Logically, all that would be left is a blank wall. When religion is removed, morality goes too.

Ironically, humanists at times do talk about morality. But when they do, they piggyback on the Judeo-Christian ethic. When they believe in human dignity, freedom and peace, they are assuming a theistic view of the world. For those of humanistic thinking were also created in God's image and were given a moral consciousness, even though they may fail to recognize its origin.

We have not yet seen the full result of humanism in the United States, because we are still coasting on the values derived from our rich Judeo-Christian heritage. But what of the generations to follow? As that heritage fades, everyone will be permitted to do whatever seems right in his own eyes in a world of twisted values, where morality is ridiculed and evil becomes a virtue. God clearly pronounces judgment on those who "call evil good, and good evil; that put darkness for light, and light for darkness" (see Isa. 5:20).

MYTH NUMBER FOUR

"Whatever Is Legal Is Moral."

At the war crimes trial in Nuremburg, Germany, Hitler's henchmen argued that they had broken no laws. Germany's own legal system, they contended, permitted the elimination of those who impeded the advance of the Third Reich. Adolph Eichmann protested before his execution, "I had to obey the laws of war and my flag."

In our own country, a group protesting an abortion clinic were charged with slander because they had called abortionists "murderers." The abortionists argued, as had the accused at Nuremberg: You can't call someone who isn't breaking a law a murderer.

Both the experience of Nuremberg and today's silent holocaust in our abortion clinics bear eloquent witness to the fact that when a state believes it is accountable to no one except itself, it assumes a hidden premise: that whatever is legal is moral.

Robert H. Jackson, chief counsel for the United States in the Nuremberg Trials, was forced to appeal to permanent values, to moral standards transcending the lifestyles of a particular society. In effect, he argued that there is "a law beyond the law" that stood in judgment on the arbitrary changing opinions of men.

Today the shape of America is being altered by use of the same strategy. The Supreme Court, influenced by the humanistic trends, has helped to brainwash our people to believe that whatever is legal is moral. They would argue that there is no law above human laws.

This is not the case of our founding fathers. Whether individually Christian or not, there was a general consensus of theism, the belief that God existed and the new republic was based upon this foundation. This understanding profoundly influenced their view of law and government.

As the Christian world view has faded, America has turned not to the laws of God, but to what Francis Schaeffer called "sociological law." Law is only what the majority wants, or what the judges say it is.

Thus in 1973 the Supreme Court invalidated the abortion laws of fifty states and legalized abortion on demand. Where did the Court get the notion that a woman has a right to an abortion? Such right is not found in the Constitution. The Court made it up. Like Napoleon, it crowned itself emperor— answerable to no one—not even the American people.

Such distortion of "rights" has also opened the doors to pornography, under the guise of a free press, and to the offense of the public at large. As Christians we must explode the myth that whatever is legal is moral.

What men make legal is not necessarily moral.

MYTH NUMBER FIVE

"Morality Cannot Be Legislated."

Secular humanists would like us to believe that they are broad-minded, pluralistic and neutral in moral matters. They are opposed to censorship, sectarianism and intolerance. The media has done a successful job of getting the American people to believe that it is the so-called right wing religious fanatics who are seeking to "impose their morality on society."

But all laws are an imposition of someone's morality. That is why the statement, "You cannot legislate morality" as it stands is absurd.

Secular humanism is imposing its own morality on the American public. It does so through the media, the schools and the courts.

There is a clear intent to keep Christian thinking out of the mainstream of the media and the nation's political life.

When Francis Schaeffer's film, *Whatever Happened to the Human Race?* was shown on a television station in Washington, pro-abortionists exerted all the influence they could to prevent it from being aired. (Liberal establishments are strangely silent about the pluralism and openmindedness they verbally espouse when the cause contradicts their own.) Even after the showing, the *Washington Post* ran an article entitled, "No Matter How Moving, Show Still Propaganda." Thus the media ridiculed the program with loaded terminology.

One editor admitted that the only religious news story that the press likes to do is a scandal.

When a book entitled, "How to Have Sex With Children," was confiscated by the Chicago police, several demonstrators marched in protest, insisting that pornographers should have unlimited privileges. But neither prayer nor a creationist view is allowed in the classroom.

As columnist George Will put it so ably, "And it is, by now, a scandal beyond irony that thanks to the energetic litigation of 'civil liberties' fanatics, pornographers enjoy expansive first amendment protection while first graders in a nativity play are said to violate first amendment values."

No law is neutral. Every law imposes some form of morality on society. Abortionists impose their morality on the unborn. Homosexuals want their views flaunted in the public school classrooms. Atheists want religious influence excluded from public life.

Some politicians, in an attempt to remain "neutral" on such issues as abortion and sidestep the flak, say they are personally opposed to abortion but would never "impose their values

on society."

If so, how does this sound?

"I personally would never gas a Jew, but I have no right to impose my moral judgment on the Nazis...I don't think the courts have the right to reach into someone's private gas chamber and legislate morality."

The question is not whether the public will allow religion to "impose its morality" on America. Morality *will* be imposed. The real question is: Whose morality will be legislated?

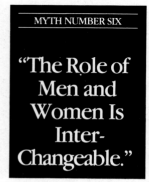

MYTH NUMBER SIX

"The Role of Men and Women Is Inter-Changeable."

On the surface it may seem that every Christian should be in favor of such legislation as the ERA. If we take seriously the biblical teaching that women are created in the image of God, they certainly are entitled to equal rights.

Yet behind the proposed amendment lies a deception. If ERA had been ratified, it would have brought a sweeping restructure of society, with devastating attack on the family and morality in general. The amendment would likely destroy America as we know it.

The radical feminists who so vociferously back the movement want, first of all, to end the institution of marriage. Sheila Cronan speaks for many of them when she writes, "Since marriage constitutes slavery for women, it is clear that the Women's Movement must concentrate on attacking this institution. Freedom for women cannot be won without the abolition of marriage."

These same feminists want freedom from the burden of children. There can

be no equality, they insist, as long as the woman is a homemaker. Moreover, the children, they say, should be reared by another, namely the state. The Houston Conference for Women, sponsored by N.O.W., called for federally-funded day care centers around the clock, seven days a week. Society as a whole, they insist, should bear the burden.

Lenin pursued this philosophy in Russia. So has Cuba. And Communist China. It is a Marxist solution.

The National Organization for Women opposes the right of churches to make any differentiation between men and women. The refusal to ordain homosexuals could soon be interpreted as "contrary to public policy," and homosexual teachers could flaunt their lifestyle in the public classroom.

Meanwhile, in an incredibly ridiculous project, even the World Council of Churches has released a Biblical Lectionary that omits all gender-based terms, including all references to God as "He."

Both the Scriptures, and the overwhelming majority of the public at large, still make clear distinctions between male and female. To disregard these differences is to invite the disintegration of America.

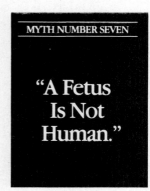

MYTH NUMBER SEVEN

"A Fetus Is Not Human."

This very day, as you read this article, some 4,300 preborn babies will legally be put to death — under the protection of the Supreme Court's 1973 decision in Roe vs. Wade.

In earlier days abortion was the last act of a desperate woman. Today it is said that 97% of all abortions occur simply for convenience. It has become the nation's means of birth control.

Wrote Peter Singer in *Pediatrics,* " We can no longer base our ethics on the idea that human beings are a special form of creation made in the image of God and singled out from all other animals." Babies' bodies have been sold by the bag. They are used in some cosmetics and for experimentation. In one general hospital, the sale of preborn babies brought in $68,000 in a ten-year period.

Justice Harry Blackman, author of the 64-page document that came from the Roe vs. Wade decision, said that objection to abortion came mainly from two sources: the oath of Hippocrates and Christianity. Since the oath specifically forbids abortion, the Court wrestled with its influence but concluded that, in the context of general opinion, "ancient religions did not bar abortion." As for Christianity, it was apparently dismissed by the court because of the separation of church and state. In effect, the Court omitted two thousand years of Judeo-Christian influence and reached back into paganism to find a basis for its moral judgment.

Those who have studied the document in detail confess that it is a mix of illogical reasoning and *nonsequiturs.* Justice Byron White dissented on the decision and said, "I find nothing in the language or history of the Constitution to support the Court's judgment."

As a result of the tragic decision, more than 18 million unborn children have had their lives snuffed out — ten times the total number of Americans lost in all of our nation's wars.

Today abortion is big business. With 1.5 million each year, at an average cost of $350 each, abortion clinics are raking in thousands of dollars daily.

How could our justices have blundered so badly? The answer: they bowed to the pressure of feminists who were calling for abortion on demand as a legitimate right. It is what happened on the bench one hundred years ago, when the *Dred Scott* decision denied the black his right to freedon and relegated blacks to the status of "nonpersons" — for personal convenience.

The decision was also the result of the "new morality" of the Sixties. Seventy-five percent of all those who have abortions are unmarried. Abortion has become the "mopping up operation" from a breakdown in moral values.

MYTH NUMBER EIGHT

"We Can Ignore the Ghost of Karl Marx."

We cannot ignore the man who rules nearly one-half of the world from his grave. The magnetic power of Marxism is unparalleled in history, impacting peoples from China to Moscow, from Cuba to Central America. "Liberation theology," so popular in Latin America, has attempted to combine some elements of Marxism with Christianity in an attempt to rectify the gross inequities that exist between rich and poor, the powerful and the weak.

Capitalism is seen as the root of all evil. Marx believed that if private property were abolished, all prejudices and injustices would vanish. Incredibly, this myth is widely believed.

In the United States, *Sojourners* magazine, with a circulation nearing 40,000, attempts to combine Christianity with a leftist political stance. It is committed to liberation theology both for Central America and the United States. Over a period of six years it has criticized numerous countries for human rights violations, but not once was a Marxist-Leninist country named. Marxist countries are always portrayed favorably; capitalistic regimes are denounced. All the while the editors claim to be expounding biblical Christianity.

It seems incredible that a system that has annihilated millions, and that continues to slaughter innocent peoples in nations like Afghanistan, should be held up as an answer to "human rights."

When Russia in 1983 shot down a Korean jetliner with nearly 400 people aboard, there was an outcry from the West. Those who did not understand Marxism expressed dismay that the Soviets would kill innocent passengers riding in what was known to be an unarmed passenger plane. But such atrocities are in perfect accord with a Marxist notion that individuals have no inherent rights — only those conferred by the state. Those who stand in the way of the state's goals can be legally eliminated.

Clearly the ghost of Marx was present when the Supreme Court gave women and absolute right to an abortion without any interference by the father or grandparents of the child. The *Roe vs. Wade* argument: "the state has no compelling interest in the life of the unborn...." Abortion was legalized because the *state* saw no reason to protect the life of the unborn.

Marxism has failed miserably, however, in part because of its defective view of human nature.

WHEN GOD LISTED THE VALIANT WARRIORS OF ISRAEL, HE ADDED A SIGNIFICANT COMMENT ABOUT THE MEN OF ISSACHAR. THEY "…WERE MEN THAT HAD UNDERSTANDING OF THE TIMES, TO KNOW WHAT ISRAEL OUGHT TO DO…." IT IS IMPERATIVE THAT CHRISTIANS APPLY THE PRINCIPLES OF GOD'S WORD IN REFUTING THE FALSE CONCEPTS OF OUR DAY.

BILL GOTHARD

Radical feminists in this country derive much of their vision from the literature of Socialism. They admit in fact, that their goals cannot be achieved in a capitalistic society. As Lenin put it, "We cannot be free if one-half of the population is enslaved in the kitchen." Nor can a country be free, says Communist doctrine, if parents have the right to teach their children religion.

When Thomas Jefferson spoke of a wall between church and state, it was intended to prevent state religion, not the Christian view. Marxist countries place a firm wall between church and state. It is permissible to have Christian ideas, perhaps, as long as these in no way spill over to the person's lifestyle in society, or his views in the public arena. This is the new understanding of the separation of church and state that is being heralded in America.

MYTH NUMBER NINE

"Pornography Is a Harmless Adult Pleasure."

Our nation is drowning in a sea of sensuality. With explicit magazines, sensual movies and video tapes readily available, we are rotting from the inside.

One-half of all divorces take place because of adultery — often encouraged by pornography.

Charles H. Keating, Jr., in a report on pornography to the U.S. Senate Judiciary Committee, reports that a recent study by the Michigan State Police, using a computer to classify over 35,000 sex crimes in that state alone over a 20-year period, found that 43 percent were pornography-related.

Pornography gives a distorted view of human sexuality. It stresses the erotic without so much as giving a hint as to where its path will lead.

No one can calculate the number of divorces, the emotional scars, the bondage and the guilt that pornography has brought to America. Only a massive effort on the part of thousands can possibly stem the rush to judgment that this plague has brought.

I am thankful for the National Federation for Decency that wages the battle against pornography. Some important gains have been made. There are cities in the United States where adult book shops have been closed because of the insistence of citizens that the laws be applied. Millions of decent citizens could, if they wished, boycott those stores where pornography is sold. Once our impact is felt, pornography could be severely restricted.

The Attorney General of the United States should receive "a blizzard of mail" requesting the enforcement of the federal law that prohibits obscene materials from moving in interstate commerce.

For many Christians the movie theatre used to be taboo. Today's generation of Christians, by and large, regard it as neutral — a place that can show good or evil. Encouraged by such films as *The Sound of Music,* our generation began to select what movies it would see. But it soon became difficult to draw the line. Christians who began to attend movies that were more risque would comment, "The movie was great...if only one or two of the scenes would have been cut." Offenses were tolerated, often with the excuse that "it was no worse than what you can see on TV."

Because of the explosive power of sexuality, that invisible line was pushed

THE REBIRTH OF AMERICA

farther and farther down the path of sensuality. Young people particularly were bound to find ways to see sexually provocative movies. Once their appetite was whetted, they became addicted. Many parents lost control of the situation with their sons and daughters, then wondered why the "looseness" in their children's moral views and behavior.

Now with the video explosion and cable TV, everything is up for grabs.

Only the people of God can arrest our slide into the cesspool of sensuality. But the question is whether we have the moral fiber to put our own house in order so that we can speak to the world.

MYTH NUMBER TEN

"The Church Should Have No Voice In Government."

In the early days of America, Christians took leadership in the government without any thought that Christianity and politics don't mix. Only after the modernist-fundamentalist controversy did fundamentalism withdraw from the political arena.

That gave the secularists a grand opportunity to entrance themselves in the political process. Thankfully, the situation is changing as Christians become more aware of their responsibility toward God in government.

We must agree with Daniel Webster that " whatever makes men good Christians makes them good citizens." As individuals we can be a part of the political process. In politics we must fight for the candidates that come the closest to the ideals that we hold, while recognizing that no one may agree with us on every issue.

Our priority, as Christians, is still the gospel. And our message must be clear: repent, or judgment of some kind is inevitable, a huge defense budget notwithstanding. We cannot apply a political solution to what is essentially a spiritual problem.

Despite such dangers, we can be thankful for groups which have inspired Christians to become active in politics. History may record that it was the participation of Christians in politics in the 1980's that awakened this nation from its slide into the abyss of moral oblivion. Nazism triumphed in Germany, at least in part, because the church voiced little opposition to Hitler's brazen political methods and calloused moral behavior. Thanks in part to the convictions, initiative and recent writings of concerned men of God, the evangelical church in America has asssumed a new vigor in the realm of politics and society.

"Humanism is not new. It is, in fact, man's second oldest faith. Its promise was whispered in the first days of the Creation under the Tree of the Knowledge of Good and Evil: 'Ye shall be as gods.' "

WHITTAKER CHAMBERS

We have all seen the statistics that reveal the breakdown of the family unit in our society...more than one out of every two couples who walk down the aisle to get married will eventually change their minds and end up in a divorce court; last year over 600,000 children were born to unmarried women; each month the lives of 125,000 children are cruelly ended before they even have a chance to leave their mother's womb; an estimated 10 million Americans are engaged in perverse, homosexual relationships.

The tragedy is that these statistics represent human lives...real people who are experiencing the consequences of refusal to follow God's plan for the family.

DEL FEHSENFELD

THE FRACTURED FAMILY

BY ARMAND NICHOLI JR.

Increasing waves of declining morality are battering our nation's families.

For several years now social scientists have warned us that the family is disintegrating and will not survive this century. Several writers have criticized the family and stated that this process of disintegration ought to be encouraged. In a book titled *The Death of the Family,* a British physician suggests doing away with the family because it is a primary conditioning device for a Western, imperialistic world view. In *Sexual Politics,* Kate Millett writes that the family must go because it oppresses and enslaves women. This idea is reflected in women's liberation literature.

Is there danger that the American family will cease to exist? I do not think so. A larger percentage of Americans marry today, have children, and commit themselves to living in a family household than ever before. We do, however, have serious cause for concern — not that the family will disappear, but that certain trends prevalent today will incapacitate the family, destroy its integrity, and cause its members to suffer such crippling emotional conflicts that they will become an intolerable burden to society.

Let's look at a few of these trends. The trend toward quick and easy divorce and the ever-increasing divorce rate subject more and more children to physically and emotionally absent parents. The divorce rate has risen 700 percent in this century and continues to rise. There is now one divorce for every 1.8 marriages. Over a million children a year are involved in divorce cases and 13 million children under eighteen have one or both parents missing.

Overworked Working Mothers.

The increasing numbers of married women who have joined the labor force and work outside of the home — especially mothers with young children — have a profound effect on family life. In 1948, 18 percent of the nation's mothers worked outside of the home. In 1971 this figure jumped to 43 percent. Today it is over 50 percent. This phenomenon has increased marital stress and contributed to the high rate of divorce. What I find most disturbing is that an increasing percentage of mothers who work have young children. Nearly 6 million pre-school children have working mothers. Only a small fraction of these mothers work because of economic necessity.

Changing Ideas About Motherhood.

Many colleges and universities convey the notion that the role of wife and mother is passe, and to settle for such a role in life is to settle for second-class citizenship. The women's liberation movement has had an impact here. Though it focuses on many legitimate grievances, it appears eager to deny the responsibility of being a wife and mother. Unless these women can pursue a career while raising a family, they consider their lives a failure. My clinical experience indicates clearly that no woman with young children can do both at the same time without sacrificing either the quality of work or the quality of child care.

. The obtrusion of television into the home has affected the North American family in ways we have not yet begun to fathom.

The Great Interrupter.

We are just beginning to experience the first generation brought up completely on television. Some studies have shown that the average viewing time of the American child from six to 16 years of age is between 20 and 24 hours per week. If he lives to be 80, and continues to watch TV at that rate, he will have spent 8 to 10 years of his life watching television. Or to put it another way, he lives about 20,000 days. One fifth of his waking life or about 4,000 days will have been spent watching television.

Uncontrolled Behavior.

The family is also affected by the lack of impulse control in our culture today. The deep moral confusion we have observed over the past decade seems to have lifted all restraint.

Aggression in the home has been increasing steadily. Since it has been required to report "battered child"

cases, we have observed an alarming increase in this phenomenon. Authorities expect between 2 and 4 million cases to be reported this year. About 15,000 of these will suffer permanent brain damage; about 2,000 will die. Many more cases go unreported.

Promiscuity and Perversion.

Even more prevalent in society is the failure to control sexual impulses. The number of illegitimate births in this country continues to rise and more than one-quarter of a million occur each year. Twenty-one percent of all births in the United States occur in the age group between 12 and 19; half of these girls are unmarried. Teenage pregnancies have increased by 33 percent within the past 5 years. Statistics for 1974 show more than one-half million teenage pregnancies, half of which terminated in abortion. That 50 percent of teenage marriages end in divorce within 5 years makes these findings no less disturbing. I have also noticed an increased incidence of homosexuality among young people and also much greater freedom in expressing it.

These trends hurt the family because they contribute to a change in child rearing that has taken place in this country during the past few decades. Child care has shifted from parents to other agencies. A home in which both parents are available to the child emotionally as well as physically has become the exception rather than the rule.

What about the future? What can we expect if these trends continue? First, the quality of family life will continue to deteriorate, producing a society with a higher incidence of mental illness than ever before. Ninety-five percent of our hospital beds may be taken up by mentally ill patients.

This illness will be characterized primarily by a lack of self-control. We can expect the assassination of people in authority to be a frequent occurrence, as well as events like the 16-year-old girl who recently began shooting people "for the fun of it." Crimes of violence will increase, even those within the family. Because battered children (if they survive) tend to become parents who abuse their children, the amount of violence within the family will increase exponentially. The suicide rate will continue to rise — mostly among teenagers and those in mid-life. In the past 20 years, however, the suicide rate in 10-to-14 year-olds has tripled. We already are producing an enormous number of angry, depressed, and suicidal kids.

We will also continue to witness changes in the expression of sexual impulses. As sexuality becomes more unlimited, more separated from family and emotional commitment, the deadening effect will cause more bizarre experimenting and widespread perversion. Jean O'Leary has written in the National Organization for Women publication that lesbianism should be taught in our schools and that school counselors should take courses "to teach a positive view of lesbianism." And a group in Boston called the Boston Boise Committee has been trying to convince the public that there is nothing "inherently wrong with sex between men and boys," to lower the age of consent to 14, and to change the child molestation laws to reduce legal barriers against such relationships.

Self Denial: Key to Fulfillment?

As a nation we appear to be more confused morally than at any time in our history. Perhaps we need to hear a little less about self-fulfillment and a little more about self-denial. Could it be that denial is a key to fulfillment?

We need to hear more about the infinite worth of a human being, that one child or one spouse transcends in time and significance all of our secular institutions put together — even our institutional churches. Parents today often resent children because they interfere with their "fulfillment."

> **Parents Today Often Resent Children Because They Interfere With Their Fulfillment.**

If a woman of 25 with two children, 2 years apart, gives full time to rearing them until they are eighteen, this leaves her with two-thirds of her adult life to follow whatever interest she desires. Is this too great a sacrifice?

We need to take time for our vertical relationship, and for relationships with members of the family, whether at home or away. Not only do they need us, but whether we realize it or not, we need them.

In our day we are seeing an all-out assault on the family. It is coming from many different sources. We must become aware of these sources so that we can wisely build a spiritual "wall of protection" around the family and use the family as a strong base to turn our nation back to God.

The family has always been the cornerstone of American society.

Our families nurture, preserve and pass on to each succeeding generation the values we share and cherish, values that are the foundation for our freedoms. In the family, we learn our first lessons of God and man, love and discipline, rights and responsibilities, human dignity and human frailty.

Our families give us daily examples of these lessons being put into practice. In raising and instructing our children, in providing personal and compassionate care for the elderly, in maintaining the spiritual strength of religious commitment among our people—in these and other ways, America's families make immeasurable contributions to America's well-being.

Today more than ever, it is essential that these contributions not be taken for granted and that each of us remember that the strength of our families is vital to the strength of our nation.

Ronald Reagan

RONALD REAGAN
THE WHITE HOUSE

THE PORNO PLAGUE

BY DAVID JEREMIAH

An onslaught of seduction has overwhelmed America:
our nation is infected with the fatal disease of pornography.

Each year, the industry that produces "adult" products of one kind or another chalks up at least $4 billion in profit. That is as much as the legitimate movie and record industries make combined. Six of the most profitable newsstand monthlies are now "male entertainment" magazines. Over 500,000 children are used as models in the "child porn" industry. A recent publication on syndicated child pornography noted that over 280 monthly publications are produced in America on that subject alone.

Pornography is one of the most unselective evil influences in our society. Gambling is restricted to adults. Tobacco is not to be sold to anyone under 18. Alcohol is not to be sold to minors. But every time your children and mine walk past the average drugstore magazine rack, the ugly demon of pornography stares out at them. Though most stores have tried to camouflage the blatant sex magazines by covering the racks, the pruriently written smut is still accessible through the paperback book racks in the back of the store.

The Illegitimate Birth of the Playboy Philosophy.

The aggressive, open marketing of pornographic sex began in 1955. Hugh Hefner, with little money and a center-page foldout of a nude Marilyn Monroe, bargained the Playboy theme into a $170 million empire — one of the most amazing financial success stories in journalistic history.

Hefner's magazine has led the way in communicating pornography through pictures and carefully planned and written articles attacking Judeo-Christian morality.

During the twenty years following the birth of Playboy, one hundred competitors followed, crowding good magazines off the newsstands. No one ever dreamed that the competition in filth would eventually excrete a magazine like *Hustler,* sold everywhere and currently boasting a serious challenge to Playboy's circulation records.

The Tarnished Silver Screen.

But the plague is not limited to the printed page alone. Can anyone deny that movies are dirtier than ever? They do not call it dirt. They call it "realism." The movie industry's announcement that perversion and homosexuality would no longer be barred from the screen, provided the subjects were handled with "delicacy and taste," opened the door for an even lower level of decency in the industry. And that which has not been barred from the screen is now no longer barred from the home either. Double and triple X-rated movies are now available through cable TV. They are being sold in stores on video cassettes and little by little are creeping into our prime time television. Children left unattended for a short time in many homes could be exposed to the rawest of pornography, just by turning the TV dial in the wrong direction.

We are drowning our young people in violence, cynicism, and sadism. Someone has observed that the grandchildren of the kids who used to weep because the little match girl froze to death now feel cheated if she is not slugged, raped, and thrown into a furnace.

The Seeds of Destruction.

One clear principle of the Word of God is this: The seeds of destruction are contained in every sin. James 1:15 puts it this way: "Then when lust hath conceived, it bringeth forth sin: and sin, when it is finished, bringeth forth death." Galatians 6:7,8 says, "Be not deceived; God is not mocked: for whatsoever a man soweth, that shall he also reap. For he that soweth to his flesh shall of the flesh reap corruption."

Someday, if she does not return to righteousness, America will reap what she has sown. Therefore, Christians must not let go unchallenged the flood of pornography that involves the exploitation of the weakness of man and the corruption of his spiritual and moral nature. Pornography makes a woman an object of lust rather than a person made in the image of God. Pornography, in attacking the image of

God in man, is an attack upon God Himself, and God will not be mocked.

Pornography's Destructive Effect on Culture.

Police vice squads report that 77 percent of the child molesters of boys and 87 percent of the child molesters of girls admitted trying out, or imitating, the sexual behavior modeled by pornography. In one group of rapists, 57 percent indicated they had tried out the sexual behavior they had seen depicted in pornography. The Michigan State Police, in a recent study of 35,000 sex crimes over a 20-year period, found that 43 percent were pornography-related.

A casual glance at the lists of the sins of the flesh recorded in the New Testament will reveal that the sins of sexual looseness are grouped together with the sins of violence. They always go hand in hand. We should not be surprised to see it today (see Rom. 1:26-31; Gal. 5:19-21; Eph. 5:3,11).

Disintegrated Judgment.

Lord Devlin, the famous British jurist, in a book entitled *The Enforcement of Morals,* wrote, "A sense of right and wrong is necessary for the life of a community. Without it the society will destroy itself. History shows that the loosening of moral bonds is the first stage of disintegration."

Destroyed Relationships.

Pornography constitutes a direct attack on significant relationships because it helps create a mind-set that eventually treats all people as sexual objects. Modern pornography is an education system. It teaches. Its message is: Human beings are mere animals; the highest value is immediate pleasure;

other people may be used and abused and then discarded. It teaches that sex is divorced from love, commitment, morality, and responsibility, that perversion is to be preferred to normality, that women are fair game for anyone who cares to exploit them.

How to Arrest the Porno Plague.

There are some things that concerned Christians can do to keep this disease from spreading any further. We can examine our cities' zoning ordinances, which might help restrict advertising and newsstand displays. We can exercise our consumer rights by not supporting publishers and producers who traffic in pornography. We can refuse to buy products produced by firms that sponsor smut shows on TV.

We can urge newspapers to restrict pornographic advertising, as the New York Times and a few other papers have done. We can speak out in disgust against those who claim to have been born again, yet continue to produce filth that belongs in the gutter.

Most of all, we can make sure that we keep ourselves unspotted by the world. With the constant bombardment facing Christians every day, more than a few have succumbed to the temptation.

Staying Pure in an Impure World.

Keeping ourselves pure before God will not come easy to modern Christians. Without a plan to deal with this

area of life, all of us are subject to defeat. Perhaps the following suggestions will help those who struggle in this matter.

1. *Covenant with your eyes.* Job did (see Job 31:1), and it's a good suggestion for all of us. The eyes provide the window to the mind. Most problems, especially for men, start here. By the power of the Holy Spirit, we can be disciplined in the use of our eyes.

2. *Consecrate your mind.* The mind is the battleground upon which every moral and spiritual battle is fought. Our thinking ultimately determines our character. Solomon said, "As a man thinketh in his heart, so is he" (Prov. 28:7). Jesus explained to His disciples that the heart was the seat of indwelling sins: "For from within, out of the heart of men, proceed evil thoughts, adulteries, fornications, murders, thefts, covetousness, wickedness, deceit, lasciviousness, an evil eye, blasphemy, pride, foolishness: All these evil things come from within, and defile the man" (Mark 7:21-23).

3. *Commit yourself to Bible memorization.* Christians are responsible for "bringing into captivity every thought to the obedience of Christ" (II Cor. 10:5). There is only one way to accomplish this goal: We must fill our minds with God's Word. The psalmist had this in mind when he wrote, "Wherewithal shall a young man cleanse his way? By taking heed thereto according to thy word...Thy word have I hid in mine heart, that I might not sin against thee" (Ps. 119: 9,11). When we have commit-

> As a Man Thinketh in His Heart, So Is He.

ted many passages of God's Word to memory, we will discover that they come to our minds, at just the right moment, to aid us in gaining victory in this battle.

4. *Counteract Satan's strategy in your life.* I am convinced that as Satan goes about seeking whom he may devour, he has a definite strategy for each of us. I am quite often surprised by the consistency of sinning Christians. Same time, same place, same companions, same circumstances, over and over again. Satan knows our weaknesses and uses all the tools at his command to keep us constantly in great spiritual jeopardy. When will we learn that there are certain places and situations that promote sin in our lives? It may be the magazine rack in the airport newsstand, the local theater, the movie channel on your TV set, the "adult" bookstore you have to pass on your way to work. Whatever it is, we must determine not to give our enemy an advantage. Stay away from the airport magazine racks, don't go to the theater, discontinue cable TV, take another route home. Don't knowingly put yourself in the place of defeat. Certainly Paul had this in mind when he wrote these words to the Romans: "Neither yield ye your members as instruments of unrighteousness unto sin but yield yourselves unto God, as those that are alive from the dead, and your members as instruments of righteousness unto God" (Rom. 6:13).

Some time ago, after preaching a message on the subject of pornography on our television program, I received this letter from a man who had watched the service many hundreds of miles away:

Dear Pastor Jeremiah,

I was sitting here in my room contemplating going out and having a beer and possibly looking upon porno flicks or whatever else the night might bring. As I was getting ready to go out, I turned on the TV and your program was being shown. I listened with great interest as you uncovered my life story. It seems almost as if you received your sermon from the files in my head.

Down deep as I search myself, I know I am doing wrong. I, at times, feel guilty about the things I do. I cannot honestly say that I enjoy getting drunk, nor do I enjoy subjecting myself to the filth that is associated with the sex market. From time to time, I find myself getting up in the middle of a triple-X movie out of sheer disgust over what I see on the screen. I am a happily married man, and I have three beautiful children. I know my wife would flip if she knew what I do when I am away from home...I feel so dirty now, and I hope somehow you can make sense out of what I've said. I have turned my back on God and sometimes I feel as though He has given up on me.

You spoke of being saved. How do you really know? Tonight I sit here with tears in my eyes, and I don't know why. Please help me if you can!

Hope and Forgiveness... For Anyone.

The message of hope for this man is the message of hope for each and every man whose life is weighed down by the sin of evil thoughts. "Come now, and let us reason together, saith the Lord: though your sins be as scarlet, they shall be as white as snow, though they be red like crimson, they shall be as wool" (Isa. 1:18). "The blood of Jesus Christ...cleanseth from all sin" (I John 1:7). That promise applies to the sin of the unclean mind.

Paul reminded the Corinthians that even though some of them had been fornicators, idolaters, adulterers, effeminate, abusers of themselves with mankind, thieves, covetous, drunkards, revilers, and extortioners, yet nonetheless, they had been washed clean "in the name of the Lord Jesus" (I Cor. 6:11).

Edmund Burke never spoke more eloquently than when he spoke of his beloved Britain:

"Men are qualified for civil liberty in exact proportion to their disposition to put moral chains upon their own appetites...Society cannot exist unless a controlling power upon will and appetite be placed somewhere; and the less of it there is within, the more there must be without. It is ordained in the eternal constitution of things that men of intemperate minds cannot be free."

For the true Christian, Jesus Christ and the indwelling Spirit provide the "inward control." But there is no evidence to suggest that enough Spirit-filled Christians live in our society to do away with the need for the "power" without; that God's laws and good government provide us.

In E.M. Blaiklock's commentary on Romans 1:26-32, he speaks to Christians' responsibility in a sexually permissive society:

"The close of this chapter is a warning to all peoples and all ages. Paul is describing a society which had abandoned God. He is diagnosing the malady from which Rome was to die, for no great nation has ever been destroyed by a foe from without which has not already destroyed itself by corruption within. Such sin carries its own penalty, its own damnation. The time is here when Christians must show, as they were called upon to do in Rome, by word, act and manner of life, their difference."

Though crude, pornography is a philosophical statement. It says: there are no rules about sex; sex is trivial; sex is for entertainment. Though debased, pornography is a theological statement. It says: there is no God who says I should limit my lust or channel my passion or give as well as get.... Pornography is anti-woman and anti-child. It is anti-marriage and anti-permanence. Thus it is profoundly anti-civilization. Since civilization is social support to the dymanics of life, pornography is anti-life.

WILLIAM STANMEYER

NO FREEDOM IS UNLIMITED

The issue of legislation governing pornography is becoming a major debate on the American scene. Shall legislation be further framed to abolish pornography, or does such legislation become censorship and a violation of civil rights?

Beware of those who say we can have no laws against pornography without endangering liberty. Under the cloak and name of liberty, the pornographers are out to *destroy* liberty.

There is no area where freedom is unlimited.

Take freedom of speech, for example.

No man has a right to slander others, nor do our laws allow him liberty to do so at will.

Freedom of speech does not give any man the right to walk onto the floor of Congress and speak his mind. His liberty is limited not only as to where he can say it but also as to what he says. This does not mean that he lacks freedom to speak, if it be done decently and in order.

Freedom of press means the liberty to publish, but it does not mean liberty to publish libelous statements. Nor has any man the right to publish another man's property, to publish stolen or copyrighted material. No man has the right to publish materials violating the privacy of others.

Can we give any man the unlimited liberty to do as he pleases? Can a man rob whenever he sees fit? Kill at will? If permitted, soon no one would have liberty. *Man's total liberty is always anarchy, and anarchy is the death of both law and liberty.*

Even liberty itself is under law.

The basic premise of American law calls for liberty of speech and freedom of press, subject to the necessary restrictions of law and order. The purpose of current legislative proposals concerning pornography is not the destruction of liberty but its furtherance.

Pornography demands a world of moral anarchy, a world in which anything and everything goes, especially if it is perverted. It is hostile to law and order itself. Pornography denies the very concept of law. It believes in a world without law and is dedicated to creating it. It must destroy liberty in order to usher in anarchy and a world without law.

The defense of our historic American system of liberty under law requires that we wage war against pornography.

"YOU DON'T HAVE TO READ IT." "YOU CAN SWITCH IT OFF IF YOU ARE OFFENDED." THESE AND OTHER CLICHES...HAVE BEEN USED TO JUSTIFY A SITUATION WHERE THE TASTES OF A SMALL MINORITY HAVE PROGRESSIVELY INFUSED THE WHOLE CULTURE. ON THE ASSUMPTION THAT NO ONE'S FREEDOM IS THEREBY IMPAIRED, VIOLENCE AND OBSCENITY FILL THE MEDIA, DESPITE THE FACT THAT THIS MATERIAL DOES NOT REFLECT THE CHOICE OF THE AVERAGE ADULT.

JOHN H. COURT

IS HOMOSEXUALITY AN ALTERNATE LIFESTYLE?

BY DAVID JEREMIAH

With a rise in "New Morality," America is becoming "New Sodom."

Homosexuality is almost as old as man. The first mention of it in recorded history concerns Lot and the well-known cities of Sodom and Gomorrah, over 4,000 years ago. The word sodomy, copulation with a member of the same sex, has become a byword for homosexuality and is obviously derived from that ancient city. Certainly there have been homosexuals in America since the early days of our country, But the militant and open flaunting of homosexual perversion is a relatively recent development.

Gays on the March.

The following are just a few of the many advances of the Gay Rights Movement in our country today:

- The "Blueboy," a magazine something like a homosexual "Playboy," is published by Donald Embinder, a 44-year-old gay publisher. At the last check, the magazine had a circulation of over 135,000.
- 39 cities, towns and counties, including Detroit, Washington, D.C., and Minneapolis, have enacted ordinances forbidding discrimination against homosexuals in jobs and housing.
- 120 major corporations, including AT&T and IBM, have announced that they do not discriminate in hiring or promoting people because they are homosexuals.
- TV and movies are treating gay themes more openly and sympathetically. ABC's hit series "Soap," for example, had two homosexual characters, one a macho football player.
- The Metropolitan Community Church, largely made up of homosexuals, is headquartered in Los Angeles and has 110 congregations and mission stations. It even sends out "missionaries" to organize new churches throughout the U.S., Canada, and Europe.
- Gay rights legislation is being sought that would elevate homosexuality to normalcy along with heterosexuality, give gays increased leverage to secure jobs on a quota basis, force the military and public schools to hire avowed homosexuals, and make it impossible for even church organizations to fire a homosexual if he or she were discovered after hiring.

What Does God Think of Homosexuality?

In light of the growth of this movement in our country, we do well to ask what the Creator thinks of these things. When God created the world, He established a fundamental distinction within the human race, reflected in the human body—"male and female created he them" (Gen 1:27; 5:2). It was God's plan for sexual relations to be in the form of man-woman union, man and wife becoming "one flesh" (Gen 2:24).

Homosexuals and their defenders, who argue that all human beings have the right to self-understanding and expression, reflect their determination to ignore God's design and replace His intended distinctions with their own desire.

Greg L Bahnsen, in his book *Homosexuality — A Biblical View,* puts this into perspective:

"Because man's sexual identity is defined by God, because his orientation is ordained by God, and because his sexual activity is circumscribed within a heterosexual marriage context, homosexuality cannot be viewed merely as a variant sexual preference or accidental variation within creation (akin to left-handedness). It is not a third natural sex or alternative sexual orientation in God's diverse world. Instead, it represents a choice, in some sense, to set one's desires and satisfy one's physical drives in a way contrary to God's appointment and creation. There is no natural homosexuality, for homosexuality is precisely a perversion of nature (understood as God's design for human relations). Homosexuals are made, not born; their disorder is developed contrary to their God-given identity, learned in opposition to the created order.

Pursued in defiance of the marriage ordinance."

We are told in God's Word that the integrity of the family is violated by homosexual behavior: "Thou shall not lie with mankind, as with womankind: it is abomination" (Lev. 18:22).

Leviticus 20:13 further underscores God's hatred for this sin: "If a man also lie with mankind, as he lieth with a woman, both of them have committed an abomination: they shall surely be put to death; their blood shall be upon them." From the Law of God, His verdict on homosexuality is inescapably clear.

In the first chapter of Romans, Paul teaches that the wrath of God is revealed from heaven against those who turn from their proper relationship to the Creator, holding down the truth of God, and practicing idolatry. Because they do this, says Paul, God gives them over to impure lusts, the dishonoring of their bodies. Men who give up God are given up by God to wander in moral pollution.

According to Paul, homosexuality is the cultural culmination of rebellion against God. It is symptomatic of a society under judgment, inwardly corrupted to the point of collapse. Paul regarded it as the evidence of degeneracy that caused God in His wrath to give up the nations.

What Should You Think of Homosexuality?

In light of the clear biblical teaching on homosexuality, what should be our attitude and position today? Below are several mandates.

1. Don't Be Put on the Defensive.

We must refuse to allow the exponents of the gay movement to put us on the defensive. It is the homosexual who has stepped out of the revealed will of God, not the heterosexual Christian. More than ever before, the moral Christian is being asked to defend himself against the unwarranted accusations of the homosexual. Someone has called their strategy "Rhetorical Terrorism." Two examples will illustrate their plan:

(A) "To be against homosexuality is to demonstrate a lack of love." C.S. Lewis once said, "To ask that God's love be content with us as we are is to ask that God should cease to be God: because He is what He is, His love must in the nature of things, be impeded and repelled by certain stains in our present character and because He already loves us He must labour to make us loveable." Love is at stake here. We must choose either to love sin or love God. If we love God, we will keep His commandents.

(B) "To judge a homosexual or his homosexuality is to be a bigot and thus displease the Lord." Viewing something as immoral is not the same as being a bigot. Is it customary to look on someone who condemns the killing of innocent people as a bigot toward murderers?

2. Don't Water Down What God Has Said.

We must refrain from any attempt to reinterpret the biblical evidence in light of our present culture. When our doctrine is adjusted by human wisdom or our examination of human behavior, we have destroyed the only authority God has given us to guide our lives. If it is possible to reinterpret Scripture to endorse homosexuality, we can make it endorse anything anyone would like to do or believe. It is important that we base our practice upon our doctrine and not our doctrine upon our practice. Our standards are defined by the Word of God. We can accept those standards or reject them, but we cannot tamper with them. What is at stake is not gay rights, but God's rights.

3. Don't Accept the Notion That Christianity and Homosexuality Are Compatible.

We must reject totally the idea that one can be a Spirit-filled Christian and a practicing homosexual at the same time. The biblical evidence will not allow that position. It is impossible to enter the Kingdom while rejecting and violating the standards of the King. We cannot maintain our Christian integrity if we condone what God condemns. To recognize a gay church as a church in the biblical sense of the word is to degrade the term "church." You might as well have churches for fornicators, adulterers, and robbers. The church is called to bring back the straying sheep. We are not called to say to the straying sheep that they are okay in their wanderings and that we ordain their devious paths as alternate lifestyles.

4. Don't Give Up the Fight Against Homosexual Activism.

We must resist as Christian citizens the attempts that are being made on the local and national levels to normalize or legalize homosexuality. It is not possible to give the militant gays what they want without sentencing millions of youth to a lifetime of misery. This is a price too high to pay. It violates the moral standards of God, is destructive to our country, and is in opposition to the best interests of our youth.

5. Don't Forget That Homosexuality Destroys Normal Family Relationships.

We must recognize the relationship between homosexuality and inadequate home life. Dominant mothers and hostile or absentee fathers are creating a predisposition toward homosexuality. Dr. Irving Bieber studied the family backgrounds of 106 homosexuals. According to his research, 81 mothers were dominating, 62 were overprotective, 66 made the homosexual their favorite child; 82 of the fathers spent very little time with their sons, and 79 fathers maintained a detached attitude toward them. The best way to stamp out homosexuality, according to Dr. Tim LaHaye, is to get back to the business of making parenthood a priority. Children raised in loving, well-disciplined homes, where mother and father are good role models for their children, rarely become homosexual.

6. Don't Reject the Homosexual But Reject His Sin.

We must reach out compassionately to those who are struggling to be free of the sin of homosexuality. Like Christ, we must have compassion on the sinner while at the same time we are condemning the sin. Dr. Melvin Anchell said that whoever decided to call homosexuals "gay" must have had a terrible sense of humor. They are lonely, guilty, often depressed people. Their only hope is Jesus Christ, and we must be His caring ambassadors to them.

It is interesting to note that in the context of the three passages in which Paul addressed the subject of homosexuality, he held out the only hope of recovery for the homosexual as being in the person of the Lord Jesus Christ.

Romans 3:23-24. "For all have sinned, and come short of the glory of God; being justified freely by his grace through the redemption that is in Christ Jesus."

I Corinthians 6:11. "And such were some of you: but ye are washed, but ye are sanctified, but ye are justified in the name of the Lord Jesus, and by the Spirit of our God."

I Timothy 1:15. "This is a faithful saying, and worthy of all acceptation, that Christ Jesus came into the world to save sinners; of whom I am chief."

The hope of the homosexual today is the same as it was in Paul's day. Jesus Christ can and will wash away any sin. The sin of homosexuality is not a stain too deep to respond to the cleansing power of his blood.

I'm very scared to die such a young man. I'd like a little more time. I lived in the fast lane. If only God will give me a break.

28-year-old victim of AIDS, TIME, August 12, 1985

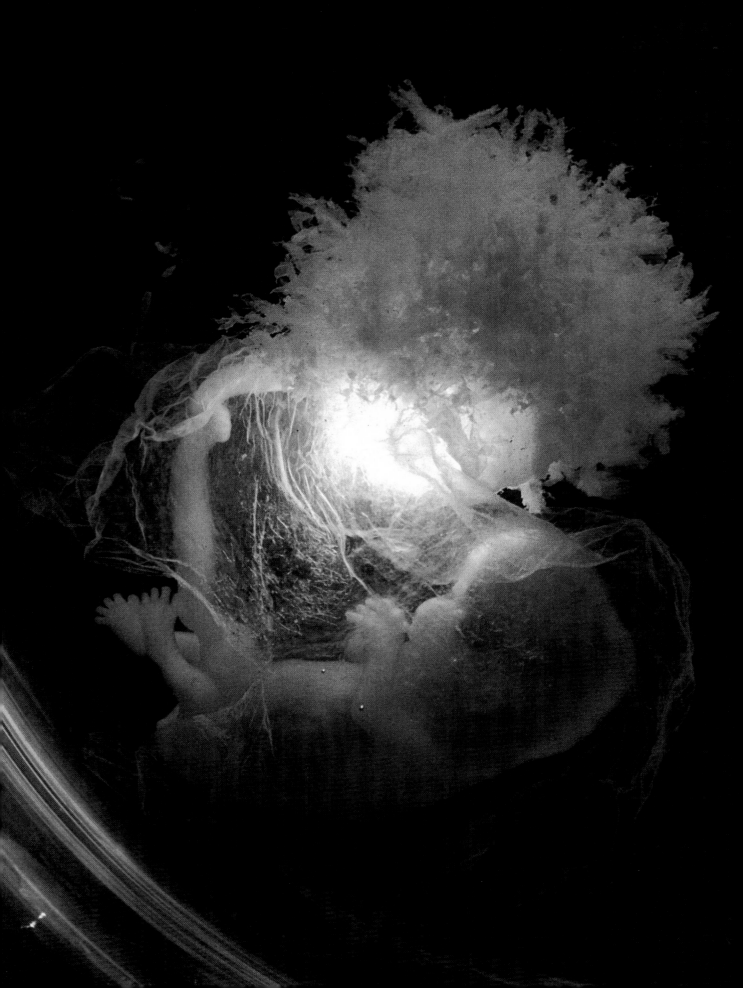

THE HIDDEN HOLOCAUST

BY ANGELA E. HUNT

*Abortion, infanticide, and euthanasia are but dominoes
in a line; abortion has fallen, infanticide is tottering,
and euthanasia may soon follow.*

"The last graves were the newest, and we started with the oldest, those of the first ghetto. In the first grave there were twenty-four thousand bodies.

"The deeper you dug, the flatter the bodies were. Each was almost a flat slab. When you tried to grasp a body, it crumbled, it was impossible to pick up. We had to open the graves, but without tools. They said, 'Get used to working with your hands.'

"When we first opened the graves, we couldn't help it, we all burst out sobbing. But the Germans almost beat us to death. We had to work at a killing pace for two days, beaten all the time, and with no tools. The Germans even forbade us to use the words 'corpse' or 'victim.' The dead were blocks of wood with absolutely no importance. Anyone who said 'corpse' or 'victim' was beaten. The Germans made us refer to the bodies as *Figuren,* that is as puppets, as dolls, or as *Schmattes,* which means 'rags.'

"The head of the Vilna Gestapo told us: 'There are ninety thousand people lying there, and absolutely no trace must be left of them.'"

—Motke Zaidl and Itzhak Dugin, survivors of Vilna, Lithuania ('Taken from *Shoah: An Oral History of the Holocaust,* by Claude Lanzmann

Recently a California company which had rented a storage cubicle fell behind on its payments; men were dispatched to clean out the facility and repossess the cubicle. What began as a simple clean-up assignment resulted in an unbelievable spectacle and bitter controversy. Seventeen thousand pre-born babies were discovered floating in formaldehyde-filled containers. The sight of so many babies, many of which were completely formed and developed to the seven and one-half month stage of pregnancy, caused many of the men to quietly withdraw and vomit.

The seventeen thousand babies were buried more than 3 years after their discovery due to the controversy which raged over whether or not they are "persons" worthy of burial. Those who opposed burial said that the containers do not contain "victims" or "corpses," but "pregnancy tissue." These seventeen thousand are the murdered "rags" and "puppets" of our generation.

Abortion. No other word is as likely to divide the American populace. Abortion advocates promote a woman's right to be child-free and her right to privacy. Those who call themselves "pro-choice" insist upon the right to an abortion for those women who bear children as a result of rape or incest, never considering that those children are worthy of the life which has already begun in them. Pre-born babies that are predicted to be deformed or "defective" are elected for termination even before the medical science which can so thoroughly explore them before birth is given a chance to help them after they enter the world.

"Strange contradictions," says Franky Schaeffer, "come forth in such times. On the one hand, we look to science and technology to solve our problems, but on the other, we place so little faith in their advance that we revert to the crudest and most archaic of all solutions—death—to solve problems." [1]

Pro-choice advocates maintain that abortion rights are absolutely necessary to prevent family tragedy. What if a woman becomes pregnant by rape? Must she bear the child of the rapist no matter what the cost to her physical and mental health? What about a young girl who bears the baby of her father? Must a victim of incest carry that baby to full term? What if pre-natal diagnosis discovers that the fetus is genetically abnormal or tragically deformed?

It is a fact: abortions in the United States for rape, incest, to protect the life of the mother, or to void a defective fetus comprise less than five percent of all abortions. Over one million babies each year are killed simply for the sake of convenience.

Rape practically never results in pregnancy. Studies in Pennsylvania and Minnesota concerning rape show that as many as five thousand rapes have occurred successively without a single pregnancy. Other studies show an incidence of none to 2.2 percent of the victims involved. Even if a pregnancy does result, an abortion does not remove the guilt or the trauma from the victim. Abortion is the same kind of violence as was the rape. [2]

One reknown surgeon remarked that in thirty-six years of pediatric surgery he has never known of one instance where the child had to be aborted to save the mother's life. [3]

Dr. Bernard Nathanson, a leading gynecologist, believes that fewer than twenty of 100,000 pregnant women will die as a result of their pregnancy. [4]

Because American lives are being prematurely snuffed out each year, the value of God-given life has been cheapened. Men have placed themselves in the place of God, deciding summarily who has "quality of life" and who does not. The weak, the infirm, those who supposedly will contribute little to society are deemed worthy of "termination."

Abortion, infanticide, and euthanasia are but dominoes in a line; abortion has fallen, infanticide is tottering, and euthanasia may soon follow.

In March 1977, at Westminster Community Hospital, California, a seven-month baby girl was born alive after a saline abortion performed by Dr. William Waddill. A nurse testified that Waddill, when he got to the hospital, interrupted her efforts to help the baby's breathing. A fellow physician testified that he had seen Waddill choke the infant. "I saw him put his hand on the baby's neck and push down," said Dr. Ronald Cornelson. "He said, 'I can't find the trachea,' and 'This baby won't stop breathing.' " Two juries, finding Cornelson an emotional and unconvincing witness, deadlocked in two separate trials. Charges against Waddill were dismissed. He had contended the infant was dying of natural causes by the time he got to the hospital. [5]

Since the 1973 Supreme Court decision allowing abortion on demand, respect for human life has declined dramatically. Infanticide is now practiced quietly in hospitals, and through the influence of the Living Will and other programs, euthanasia will become accepted and perhaps even mandatory. What can stop the holocaust of our generation?

"A hue and cry arose after the Second World War," says Franky Schaeffer, "because the railroad tracks to Auschwitz were never bombed by the allies, even though they knew that hundreds of thousands of Jews and Slovaks were being transported by them to their deaths. I wonder how future generations (if there are any) will regard those of us with Judeo-Christian principles today if we do not respond to the holocaust in our own time. The insanity of the social engineers and the purveyors of economic final solutions *must be stopped.*" [6]

We must not be silent when innocent lives are taken through abortion. We must actively fight against legislation which cheapens any aspect of human life. But first, and most important, when we hear the distorted language which could easily lull us into false security and false values, we must not believe.

"The first transport from Czestochowa was sent away on the day after Yom Kippur. The day before Succoth, there was a second transport...I was together with them. I know in my heart that something is not good, because if they take children, if they take old people, they send them away, that means it is not good. What they said is they take them away to a place where they will be working. But on the other hand, an old woman, a little child of four weeks or five years, what is work? It was a foolish thing, but still, we had no choice—we believed in them."

ABRAHAM BOMBA, SURVIVOR OF TREBLINKA

WE CANNOT DIMINISH
THE VALUE OF ONE
CATEGORY OF HUMAN
LIFE—THE UNBORN—
WITHOUT DIMINISHING
THE VALUE OF ALL HUMAN
LIFE....THERE IS NO CAUSE
MORE IMPORTANT.

PRESIDENT RONALD REAGAN

TELEVISION: THE MENACING MEDIUM

BY RON JENSON

Today's television programming is massively polluting the open fields of America's mind.

Click. The mother of a family of four flips the "on" button and the TV set glows to life. The entire family gathers for an evening of entertainment.

As the evening progresses, the family views one show where a man and woman meet at a society affair. He becomes uproariously drunk and they proceed to her apartment. By the time she can fix a cup of coffee, he has staggered into the bedroom, shed his clothes and collapsed into bed. The woman, with the steaming coffee pot in hand, surveys the scene, then returns the coffee pot to the stove.

Wordlessly she glides back into the bedroom. A zipper whispers and the woman's dress slips to the floor. The eye of the camera zooms in on the woman's back as the rest of her clothes fall to the floor. She slides into bed with her guest and softly runs her hands through his hair. The man awakes, embraces her and...

At the conclusion of the program, click, click, click. Another channel, another story. This time the entertainment centers around a model young man, whose life goes haywire. He ascends a tower at a university campus and methodically begins killing people with a high-powered rifle. One body after another crumples into a lifeless heap. Students scream in pain. Everyone else runs for cover. Finally, a sharpshooter zeroes in on the sniper and ends his hail of death with a bullet in the skull.

Click, click, click. Another channel, another program. But first a word from our sponsor. A catchy jingle about "designer jeans" is accompanied by scenes of a well-proportioned woman tightly clad in the sponsor's product. She's laughing. She's being pursued by a handsome man. She's having a good time. The obvious conclusion: wearing this product makes you sexy, attractive and popular.

Now it's time for a popular situation comedy. In this particular episode the main character lies and bluffs his way out of a sticky problem with his wife that was caused by another earlier lie. His situational ethics have ensnared him.

The scenario I have described takes place night after night in home after home across America. The names of the programs, the characters and the advertisements may differ, but the menu of violence, sex and situational ethics remains the same.

The Incredible Influence of Television.

Not all television programming is bad. But a large portion of the prime-time programming is thoroughly saturated with humanistic values. And with TV's pouring their images into homes at an average of six hours a day, can they help but make an impact on people's thinking?

Advertisers feel they can effectively promote cars, toothpaste, clothes, mouthwash, detergent and a constellation of other products. The advertisers feel that in 30-to-60-second bursts on television, they can make a difference in their sponsor's sales.

If advertisers can make a difference with such short segments, think of the impact of six-plus hours of programming per day can make!

Many of the views expressed during this time are humanistic in nature. In keeping with the "non-theistic" belief, God is largely ignored. Humanism's concept of no absolutes shows up frequently in the situational ethics of some of television's main characters. And humanism's idea of sexual conduct being unrestricted is reflected in the large amount of play given to sexual themes.

Harvard University's Project on Human Sexual Development did a comprehensive study of television's role in the sexual education of children. Their study revealed some interesting patterns in programming:

—70% of all allusions to intercourse occurs between unmarried couples or involves a prostitute;

—Much of television's erotic activity involves violence against women.

The television medium is also a strong promoter of alcohol. Television characters drink 3.5 times per hour on television, four times an hour during prime time. For every time coffee is consumed on TV, alcohol is consumed ten times. For every time milk is consumed, alcohol is consumed 44 times. For every time water is drunk, alcohol is drunk 48 times.

Of course, the media cannot bear the full blame for the alcoholism rate in this nation. But the fact that it so constantly places alcohol before the consumer, and presents it in such an alluring context (i.e., drinking is macho, drinking makes you sexually attractive, you have a good time when you drink, etc.) cannot help but influence people to drink.

> "TV May Be a Training Course in the Art of Inattention."

Television Viewing Habits of the Average American.

Academic performance may also be affected by heavy TV viewing. While the experts continue to debate its effects, some alarming facts have been accumulated. By age 18, the average American has spent an estimated 15,000 hours in front of the set, far more time than in school.

In Bedford, Mass., psychologist Thomas Mulholland and Peter Crown, a professor of television and psychology at Hampshire College, have attached electrodes to the heads of children and adults as they watched TV. While viewing TV, the subjects' output of alpha waves increased, indicating they were in a passive state as if they were "just sitting quietly in the dark." The implication: "TV may be a training course in the art of inattention," they suggest.

Groups of several hundred three- and four-year olds have been studied as they watch TV at home and in nursery school. The researchers, Professors Jerome and Dorothy Singer, who head Yale University's Family Television Research Center, are convinced that heavy TV viewing stunts the growth of imagination in the crucial ages between three and five. Such children make up fewer games and imaginary playmates.

According to other studies, by age 15 the average American child witnesses between 11,000 and 13,000 acts of violence on TV. At the moment, the debate rages among the experts about the implications of such a barrage on a child's moral sensitivities.

Television's Transmissions to the Mind.

The question of how much the humanistic ideals presented by the media affect the actions of people who view it is hard to put into statistics. The Bible says, "As a man thinketh in his heart so is he." So as people think of the amorality and sexual license presented in the media and continue to expose themselves to these ideals, their actions will be affected.

The media cannot continue to spew forth filth, immorality, violence and illicit sex into our living rooms without disastrous consequences. The media has incredible influence in our society and it must be changed.

And until it does change, we must carefully monitor our own television watching habits. Otherwise, we will see our own thinking subtly pressed into the world's mold instead of the mold set before us by the example of the Son of God.

Try going a week without television. You'll probably find its effect on you has been similar to a powerful drug. You might even sense some "withdrawal pains." But you will find that you have much more opportunity for quality time with your family and for other interests. A long-term result might be that you decide to scale down your television-viewing time in favor of other worthwhile activities.

***

A California survey indicates that the more a student watches television, the worse he does in school. California Schools Superintendent Wilson Riles said that no matter how much homework the students did, how intelligent they were or how much money their parents made, the relationship between TV and test scores was practically identical.

THE ASSOCIATED PRESS, OCTOBER, 1980

WHAT'S HAPPENED TO AMERICAN EDUCATION?

BY D. JAMES KENNEDY

In the war for our nation's children, the classroom has become the enemy's battleground.

To whom do your children belong? You would probably say that that question is patent. Obviously they belong to you. But, my friends, you should be aware of the fact that there is a growing number of people in this country who believe that that is not the way it ought to be; that indeed the children should belong and do belong to the state; and that it is their prerogative, privilege and responsibility to care for them, educate them, and mold them into proper citizens of that state.

It is this thinking and the other ideas attendant upon it that have caused something drastic to happen in the whole American educational system. I suppose everyone in America knows that there is something amiss with our educational system today. When books like *Why Johnny Can't Read* become best sellers; when it becomes common knowledge that for almost 15 years our S.A.T. scores (the achievement scores of high school students) have been going down every year; when many people who are involved tell us that our public schools have become moral jungles, and some teachers actually fear for their lives; something is amiss in our educational system.

Many people do not really know what has happened and why. I would like to take a look with you at where we have come and how we arrived there.

American Education: It Came Over on the Mayflower.

It might be well to consider where we began. Our educational enterprise in this country began, I suppose, aboard the Mayflower. Shortly before the Pilgrims set foot upon this land, they signed the Mayflower Compact in which they stated that they would create schools in order that their children might be taught to read the Word of God. Today it is unlawful for children in our public school system to read the Word of God. We, indeed, have come a long, long way. For two hundred years after the Pilgrims landed in 1620, the education of our children was in the hands of the parents or the churches. There was no such thing as public education or state education.

Why Johnny Can't Read McGuffey.

Everyone is familiar with McGuffey's Readers. William Holmes McGuffey authored *The New England Primer* and *McGuffey's Eclectic Reader* (which, by the way, sold 120 million copies) that for many decades provided the backbone of grammar school education for this country. In that Reader, McGuffey said, "The Ten Commandments and the teachings of Jesus Christ are not only basic but plenary." Is it any wonder that in the midst of our secularist educational system today, McGuffey's Readers are so anathematized! That is the way it was.

State Education, the Secular Savior.

Then in the 19th century, state education came into existence. It was public education, paid for by tax dollars with compulsory laws requiring the education of the children by the state. Slowly the various private academies and Christian schools went almost out of existence. State education took over almost completely. A little reflection on the part of a thoughtful person reveals that if the state takes over education, it inevitably leads to the fact that education itself becomes secular and statist in nature. That is precisely what our educational system has become.

In the 20th century, this education took an ominous turn. Modern progressive education was introduced and spread out across this country. The great architect of that new movement was John Dewey at Columbia Teachers College where thousands of teachers were trained. Many people when they think of progressive education think of some sort of methodology of teaching which may be somewhat different. But they fail to see that beneath the methodology is something vastly more important and that is the ideology, or, if you will, the theology that underlies the modern progressive educational movement.

It is a movement which Dewey described as a "Copernican revolution" which would produce in the educational realm a transformation which was as vast as the Copernican revolution produced in astronomy. What was the nature of that revolution? Very simply, it was this: It would produce an educational system where, instead of having God at the center, we would have man, and thus "humanism" gradually became the dominant ideology of the American public school system. Just what does that mean? Our schools are working feverishly to produce the perfect humanist man. And just what is a "humanist?" Let me give it to you in the words of the American Humanist Association itself. In their brochure, they quote Sir Julian Huxley, one of this century's leading humanists and former first head of UNESCO, thus: "I use the word 'humanist' to mean someone who believes that man is just as much a natural phenomenon as an animal or plant: that his body, mind and soul were not supernaturally created but are products of evolution, and that he is not under the control or guidance of any supernatural being or beings, but has to rely on himself and his own powers."

Atheism, American Style.

Humanism is nothing other than the American version of atheism, which positively says, "We believe in", rather than negatively, "We don't believe in God". But my friends, it is the same old thing. It is pure, unadulterated atheism with all of the resultant effects of atheism. There is no Deity. As the Humanist Manifesto itself said: "No deity will save us: we must save ourselves."

One of the inevitable results of humanism or atheism is the demise of all eternal standards or truths. Lynd, when he summarized the philosophy of

Dewey, says that the first principle of Dewey's thought was that there are no eternal truths. This is incredibly important to keep in mind. There are no eternal truths! All is relative...all is changing ...everything is in flux in the great continuum, the great change that always goes on...there are no eternal verities... there are no moral standards.

For Dewey, everything was in constant change. But it was a certain kind of change. There was a hidden agenda, there was a hidden set of values, that Dewey had and that change always had to go in a certain direction. It was a change which was understood as a rebellion against religion, against capitalism, and against individualism, and always in the direction of the collectivist socialist state. This is the underlying ideology behind the modern progressive educational system and it is unquestionably anti-Christian in its nature.

A Modern-day Titanic?

If this is the Copernican revolution in education what has it produced? Dr. W. P. Shofstall, who is the state superintendent for public schools in Arizona, in 1973 said: "The atheists have, for all practical purposes, taken over public education in this country." This does not mean that there are not still many fine Christian people laboring diligently and indefatigably in the public school system, often placing their jobs on the line by teaching the things about moral standards and God. But, unfortunately, this is very much like putting band-aids

> "The Atheists Have Taken Over Public Education in This Country."

on people on the deck of the Titanic. The results have been catastrophic.

"That our children might read the Word of God," said the pilgrims—and now the Word of God is proscribed in our public schools. "The teachings of Jesus are not only basic but plenary"— and now the teachings of Jesus are outlawed. And God, Himself, has been expelled from our public school system and banished from the school yard.

Clarifying "Values Clarification."

Today we have no eternal truths; therefore, no moral absolutes. And the results of that have been incalculable. What we have instead of moral absolutes is "values clarification." Just this week I read one of the modern texts on "values clarification" used in our public schools.... That is indeed an eye-opening experience. It says that since there are no eternal truths which are valid for this generation and succeeding generations, everybody has to find his own values in his own time. Since there is nothing which is right and wrong for everybody, there are no absolutes.

I think about that very apt verse in the book of Judges, when chaos ruled the earth: "Every man did that which was right in his own eyes." That is what we are mass-producing today in our public school system. Instead of the Bible, we now have policemen in the halls of our schools. Muggings, robberies, rapes, and even murders are commonplace in the school system today. Drug use is endemic. Alcoholism is rampant. For

THE REBIRTH OF AMERICA

college students, the two major causes of death are suicide and murder. High school pregnancies, abortions, and VD are major problems.

There are about 600,000 pregnancies carried through to term in high school age girls today in our country, which is an average of 12 unwanted children per high school per year. This does not count all of the abortions, because the student can drop out of school for a day, have an abortion, and be back again. But 12 births per high school per year! I thought of our Westminster Academy which has been open for 9 years. At the above rate 108 illegitimate children should have been born—our actual score is zero. That would seem to say something to somebody about the nature of the sex education, for example, that is given. Some people think we are opposed to all sex education. We have sex education in about a half dozen different classes at Westminster Academy. There is nothing wrong with a proper education for children in the matters of sex. It is absolutely essential. The problem with sex education in the public schools is that it is based on a completely amoral, or immoral foundation wherein there is no moral standard given to the children at all. Married sex and unmarried sex are equally all right. Heterosexual and homosexual activities are also endorsed. There are no standards for the young people.

What is the answer to our humanistic, secular public school system? They say the answer to this tremendous problem (600,000 illegitimate children among high school age girls per year) is more sex education of their amoral type or immoral type! Furthermore, they suggest more instruction and easier access to all sorts of contraceptives, abortion information, and free abortion clinics. Of course if they had their way, the parents would not have any knowledge of these things at all. Other such ideas are the only thing that the godless portion of our society can do about immorality. I think that is absolutely tragic and our children are reflecting the disastrous results of this system.

Enough Is Enough!

I cannot help but remember the words of the Scripture as I think of this great Copernican revolution where God was to be banished from our schools and this glorious new system was to come to pass with marvelous education and a wonderful new society—and where instead we have a moral jungle and an academic nightmare. The Scripture says: "The fool hath said in his heart, 'There is no God.'" I think that it is time that American parents stood up and said, "Enough! We have had enough!"

One woman went to her son's school to speak to the teacher. She had heard something about the new social studies textbooks, or a series of them called "The Promise of America." The teacher was a bit embarrassed and finally said, "We don't show some textbooks to parents." The woman said that she felt a little bit bad about it, but when all the students were out at recess, she went in and borrowed her son's textbook. She read it and was astounded! No wonder they do not show those textbooks to parents! It was filled with all sorts of profanity and blasphemy and obscenities—gutter language. It endorsed illicit sex, sex out of marriage, homosexuality and abortion. It dragged the church and God in the mud, it was unpatriotic, it recommended draft dodging, and a number of other "wholesome values" that were being taught to our children. Yet, most of the parents are completely oblivious to the whole thing.

What can be done? I am not sure. I am on a national committee which is trying to help get prayer back into the public schools. This I would like to see happen, but I must confess that deep down I have a sneaking suspicion that it is somewhat like putting a band-aid on a cancer patient. It was true that at one time we had prayer and Bible reading in our schools, but we also had a basic theistic world view. I wonder what prayer is going to mean in a school which is basically atheistic and humanistic in every phase of its teaching; where man is just an animal; where there is no Deity who can save us, and we must save ourselves. I wonder if prayer is going to mean very much in that kind of setting. It might be somewhat like opening up the evening session at the local bar with a word of prayer. I am not so sure how meaningful that might be. Nevertheless, we will try.

Have We Reached the Point of No Return?

It seems, however, that far greater transformations are needed. We need a Copernican revolution again that is going to place things as they ought to be and put God back into the center of American education. Either that is going to be done in the public school system, because of the outcry of parents and the pressure they are going to put upon the Congress of the United States, or else, I think, that the whole system should be abandoned and be allowed to sink in its own filth. I wonder if at this point it is possible to change that system back again. It may be, I don't know. I am willing to try.

I think the only answer is a return to the historic root of education in America which was parentally-controlled education or church-controlled education, where the Commandments of God and the teachings of Jesus were basic to the educational function and everything was seen in the light of the Creator of this universe. I thank God that the Christian school movement is growing faster than any other educational movement in America. There are three Christian schools being opened every single day. This is tremendously encouraging and threatening to the established humanist educational system.

Impact of the Christian School Movement.

An article in a monthly periodical, which goes out to school administrators in the public school system, analyzed this whole phenomenon of Christian school growth and they expressed great concern about it. They likened Christian schools to Amish schools, obviously going to take our children back into the 18th century or something like that, have them riding in wagons with horses. That is the kind of picture they would like to present of what Christian education is; that this is obviously something so extraordinarily backward

> I Think the Only Answer Is a Return to the Historic Root of Education in America.

and educationally so deficient that they are trying to pass all sorts of laws against it. Of course, the truth of the matter is that academically Christian education is so far superior to the public school education that there is no comparison. The grade scores indicate this and they full well know it.

It is interesting in this article, comparing the Christian schools to the Amish schools, that the author concludes that it is the right of anybody to live in the 19th century if he wants to, to march resolutely to another drummer into the past, but he says he seriously questions if they have the right to take a significant proportion of the children of America with them. We are right back to where we began. To whom do the children belong? There is a growing movement saying that these parents have no right to take their children back into the past; to march backward while the rest of America is marching forward.

Does that not sound wonderful? But look at the facts. In the very same article, in the same column, he points out that he interviewed 91 families who had children in Christian schools and he noticed a curious fact: that 89 of those 91 families had never had a divorce, which was remarkable in light of the fact that in the general society it was 1 out of 2. He didn't quite know what to do with that. While the rest of America is marching forward with 600,000 unwanted births among high school students...by innumerable hundreds of thousands of abortions...by endemic and epidemic drug use...alcoholism... suicide...and immorality of every sort... while we are marching forward into that brave new world, the Christian schools are teaching people about the moral standards of God and producing young people that love the Lord their God and desire to follow His commandments and serve Him; who love their country and are willing to serve it; who can read far better than the students coming out of the public schools and are academically superior to them—yes, indeed, my friends, there ought to be a law!

Prayer.

"Father, help us to know that to each of us as parents, there is placed upon us the responsibility of bringing up our children in the nurture and admonition of the Lord. May we take seriously Thy admonition that our children should be continually taught that which is true, in church, at home, and in school, for the glory of Thy name. Amen."

I AM MUCH AFRAID THAT SCHOOLS WILL PROVE TO BE GREAT GATES OF HELL UNLESS THEY DILIGENTLY LABOR IN EXPLAINING THE HOLY SCRIPTURES, ENGRAVING THEM IN THE HEARTS OF YOUTH. I ADVISE NO ONE TO PLACE HIS CHILD WHERE THE SCRIPTURES DO NOT REIGN PARAMOUNT. EVERY INSTITUTION IN WHICH MEN ARE NOT INCREASINGLY OCCUPIED WITH THE WORD OF GOD MUST BECOME CORRUPT.

MARTIN LUTHER

THE U.S. GOVERNMENT: MASTER OR SERVANT?

Once upon a time the people controlled the Government.
Perhaps the Government is changing that.

The legitimate purpose of government since the founding of America has been to protect the lives, liberty, and property of its citizens. James Madison summed it up well when he said, "We have staked the whole future of American civilization, not upon the power of government, far from it. We have staked the future of all of our political institutions upon the capacity of each and all of us to govern ourselves, to control ourselves, to sustain ourselves according to the Ten Commandments of God."

Our founding fathers based our system of government on the First Commandment, "Thou shalt have no other gods before me." They understood that man was created to serve God, not the state. Since man was created in God's image, government, they reasoned, should be an aid to help secure man's God-endowed rights. They instituted a system of representative government with clear limits upon what government could and could not do. This was carefully and meticulously carried out to ensure individual freedom.

Since the founding of our nation the goal of institutionalized government has been to be a servant of mankind, never the master of man. The framers of our Constitution advocated that people govern themselves under God's laws. Government should never have the power to deprive individuals of rights that the Constitution stated were "endowed by their Creator." The Declaration of Independence states that governments derive "their just Powers from the Consent of the Governed," and that "whenever any Form of Government becomes destructive of these Ends, it is the Right of the People to alter or to abolish it...."

Today we find that government is threatening our basic freedoms. Currently, more than 40 percent of a citizen's income is disposed of on his behalf by the government at the federal, state, and local levels. As late as 1928 federal governmental spending amounted to only 3 percent of the national income.

In his book *The Sum of Good Government,* U.S. Representative Phillip Crane quotes Dr. Roger Freeman: "By its massive entry over the past two decades into the field of domestic public services, the national government has decisively altered the nature of the American federal system. In establishing a federal structure with an intricate system of checks and balances, the founding fathers had aimed to disperse authority so widely that no one branch or level of government—and no one man—could prevail over the others. They concluded from history that concentration of power corrupts and sooner or later leads to abuse and tyranny. Whenever the wisdom of the age-old lesson is disregarded, its truth is brought home to the nation sooner or later with a brutal shock...American society has strayed far from its beginnings. Instead of desiring freedom from governmental interference; instead of looking to the government primarily as a source of protection from foreign or domestic enemies and not as the provider of services and benefits, Americans have embraced the very centralized government the founding fathers urged them to fear and hold in check."

We have allowed government to become all-powerful today as we have foolishly exchanged freedom for security. Economist Milton Friedman points out, "The economic controls that have proliferated in the United States in recent decades have not only restricted our freedom to use our economic resources, they have also affected our freedom of speech, of press, and of religion."

We must awake to the fact that we have been educated to dependence rather than to liberty, that we have been brainwashed by television and books to believe that it is the responsibility of government to take resources from some and bestow them upon others. Why have we done this? U.S. Senator Jesse Helms provides the answer, "When you have men who no longer believe that God is in charge of human affairs, you have men attempting to take the place of God by means of the Superstate. The Divine Providence on which our forefathers relied has been supplanted by the Providence of the All-Powerful State. I believe that this is the source of deep weakness in America, because it is a transgression of the first and greatest of the Ten Commandments."

THE HISTORY OF LIBERTY IS A history OF LIMITATIONS OF GOVERNMENTAL POWER, NOT THE INCREASE OF IT. WHEN WE RESIST, THEREFORE, THE CONCENTRATION OF POWER, WE ARE RESISTING THE POWERS OF DEATH, BECAUSE CONCENTRATION OF POWER IS WHAT ALWAYS PRECEDES THE DESTRUCTION OF HUMAN LIBERTIES.

WOODROW WILSON

FREEDOM OF RELIGIOUS EXPRESSION: FACT OR FICTION?

BY JOHN W. WHITEHEAD

Outright persecution of Christian liberty is permeating our society. Christians are called to recognize these attacks, and repel them with stalwart biblical action.

Christians have the remarkable message of Christ's Gospel to proclaim to the world. Unfortunately, that message is being increasingly stifled and censored.

We live in a nation whose founders considered free speech and free exercise of religion so important that they deliberately sealed their protection in the First Amendment of the Constitution. Today, however, Christians, and other religious persons, are being victimized by a determined, powerful secularistic effort to suppress both of those freedoms.

Secularism.

Suppression and censorship are the logical consequence of the predominance of secularism in the twentieth century. Secularism is the philosophy which holds that belief in morality is based solely in regard to the temporal well-being of mankind to the exclusion of any belief in God. All supernatural manifestations are seen as irrelevant. Since there is no God, then obviously there is no need for the moral absolutes of the Bible. All is relative.

This differs radically from the belief system which served as the historical foundation for freedom. At one time, the predominant worldview was that there was a Creator who established moral absolutes. The Creator, in turn, gave to man such absolute rights as "life, liberty and the pursuit of happiness."

This was the Christian base. It included the concept of man's createdness. Since man was believed to have been created in the image of God, he acquired, in a reflective manner, the characteristics of God. This afforded man great worth and dignity. Unfortunately, man's worth and dignity have been greatly diminished in modern society. This is best seen in the reckless disregard for human life as manifested in abortion, infanticide, euthanasia and genetic engineering.

The second key component of the Christian base was that rights were seen as an endowment from the Creator and, as a result, were absolute. Thus, rights were not a product of the state. Government, then, could not legitimately take away what God gave and government had not given.

Third, the purpose of the state was to protect the God-given rights of men. As the Declaration of Independence proclaims, whenever a government systematically attacks or attempts to destroy these rights, "it is the right of the people to alter or abolish it."

This was the base for political freedom in America. However, as the freedoms we enjoy have been separated from the Christian base, the distorted and perverted remnants have become a force of destruction.

This was illustrated early on by the French Revolution. Those who led the revolution in France in the late eighteenth century based much of their thinking on principles drawn from the Declaration, absent the Christian base. The result was a blood bath and tyranny.

We face the same possibility today. Many of those who head the modern technological elite openly attack the Christian base. Many of those who lead the news media also do this.

A representative of the new secularistic ethic is Dr. Francis Crick. He is an avowed atheist who, along with James D. Watson, discovered the DNA code. In a speech Crick made in March 1971 in St. Louis, he said:

"You must realize that most of the political thinking of this country is very difficult to justify biologically. It was valid to say in the period of the American Revolution when people were oppressed by priests and kings, that all men were created equal. But it doesn't have biological validity. It may have some mystic validity in a religious context, but...it's not only biologically not true, it's also biologically undesirable...We all know, I think, or are beginning to realize, that the future is in our hands, that we can, to some extent, do what we want."

Harvard behaviorist B.F. Skinner clearly holds that man is nothing more than a cog in a machine. He writes: "Life, liberty, and the pursuit of happiness are basic rights. But they are the rights of the individual and were listed as such in a time when the literatures of freedom and dignity were concerned with the aggrandizement of the individual. They have only a minor bearing on the survival of a culture."

If these comments were found in a comic strip, we could laugh at them. But Crick and Skinner are giants of their times, and when they speak, people listen to them. Their ideas and philosophy have consequences. Moreover, they speak for many other leaders of the technological elite.

Their philosophy is a complete repudiation of what the framers of the Declaration and the drafters of the Constitution believed. It means essentially that there is no Creator and that man has only relative rights. Also, it means that the elite (those who control the state or government) often administer government, not for the benefit of the governed, but to manipulate the country for their ends, often under the guise that they are doing it for our good. As Crick said, "We can do what we want"—that is, so to speak, they can play God.

There are, therefore, some apparent dangers in the predominance of secularism in American society and its adoption by our governmental systems. First, there is little tolerance by a secularistic state for theistic religion. As a consequence, persecution, either open or subtle, of Christianity is inevitable. Persecution is presently being manifested by such things as the growing state interference in churches, Christian schools and other Christian institutions.

Second, as Professor Harvey Cox of Harvard University has recognized: "Secularism is not only indifferent to alternative religious systems, but as a religious ideology it is opposed to any other religious systems. It is therefore, a closed system." Moreover, Cox notes that secularism is a dangerous ideological system because it "seeks to impose its ideology through the organs of the State." Because secularism has little or no tolerance and is opposed to other religions, it actively rejects, excludes and attempts to eliminate Christianity from meaningful participation in society. Its proponents must, therefore, censor and suppress Christianity. This is a logical extension of secularism.

Examples of Suppression.

Whenever Christians publicly express their views, the secularists are often waiting with regulations, lawsuits and, in some cases, even criminal charges and handcuffs. Unfortunately, their weapon in enforcing censorship is often the Constitution itself.

Consider, for example, the following recent situations.

At a public high school in Lake Worth, Florida, the principal forbade a student Bible club to meet on campus—even though the students met voluntarily and after school hours. The principal's insistence on what he perceived to be the "separation of church and state" was graphically illustrated when he ordered the Bible Club's page removed from the school's just-printed yearbook.

In Georgia, Mr. and Mrs. Terry Roemhild were arrested after they withdrew their children from public school in order to teach them at home. In spite of their religious convictions, and in spite of the evidence that the children were being well-educated at home, a Superior Court judge found them guilty of *criminal* charges, levied a fine and ordered them to re-enroll their children in public school.

A Navy man in Virginia was threatened with possible court-martial when commanding officers charged that some of his religious activities were disruptive and in violation of direct military orders. Those activities included playing a Christian radio station, reading his Bible and talking to others about his religious beliefs.

Because of her Roman Catholic convictions, a nurse in Delaware refused employment with an abortionist. In response to her refusal to aid in the killing of life, the state promptly terminated the woman's unemployment compensation benefits.

A Christian Manifesto, written by the internationally respected scholar Francis Schaeffer, sold more than 300,000 copies in just one year. Yet the book never appeared on any "secular" bestseller lists (such as the *New York Times, Newsweek,* etc.). It was never reviewed by the literary critics of any major newspapers or magazines. In fact, while Dr. Schaeffer's writings have sold more than three *million* copies, many

> # Simply Put, Early Christians Saw God at Work in the Whole Culture—Not Merely in the Heart of Man.

"secular" bookstores and libraries seem loathe to stock his books.

In Louisville, Nebraska, seven fathers were jailed for violating a court order to cease operation of a small church school. The state demanded that the school submit to state accreditation. The parents, along with the church pastor, believed that the government has no right to interfere with a church-operated school. The pastor has already been jailed several times for resisting state regulation, and just one year earlier the sheriff actually padlocked the church door to close down the school set up in the basement.

In Pawtucket, Rhode Island, the ACLU sued the city to remove a nativity scene from its elaborate Christmas pageantry, thus leaving only so-called "secular" displays to celebrate the holiday. Throughout the nation, public school teachers and administrators have been warned that holding Christmas programs with any *religious* content is strictly forbidden by the First Amendment.

To demonstrate God's condemnation of the killing of human life, David and James Henderson picketed an abortion clinic in Jacksonville, North Carolina. Two physicians—including the head of the clinic that aborts 8 to 10 unborn children *every* day—took the brothers to court in a $200,000 libel lawsuit.

Two college students in Georgia were arrested for disturbing the peace when they picketed an abortion clinic in downtown Atlanta. The charges were dropped, but one of the men was nearly fired from his job when his employer said the arrest "reflected negatively" on the organization he works for.

In Louisiana, the state legislature passed the Balanced Treatment Act, requiring public schools to give equal time to the teaching of evolution and creation-science. Many Louisiana legislators believed that academic freedom would be furthered if students were given the scientific evidence to substantiate *both* views. The ACLU, however, sued the state, insisting that creation has no scientific merit and that to include it in school curriculums would be an unconstitutional establishment of religion.

These cases represent just a scant cup of water in the sweeping tide of censorship threatening to *drown* the Christian voice. Many secularists—often backed by the potency of legislative and judicial action—are fighting to remove *all* religious expression from our public society. We have seen by these examples that their methods are varied:

"Selective" distribution and publicizing of books;

Economic penalties (as in the case of the nurse being denied unemployment compensation);

Intimidation through lawsuits or criminal charges;

Outright discrimination (as in the case of public schools allowing other clubs to meet while banning religious clubs);

State regulation (as in the case of Nebraska demanding church-school accreditation);

Absolute censorship, often under the guise of "separation of church and state."

Through laws and actions that would probably make our founders rear up in defiance, our First Amendment freedoms are being taken away. More than our speech and religious activity, however, is being censored. Abortion is the abhorrent censorship of life itself.

The Christian Silence.

But there is another side to the stifling of religious and moral expression. The repressive efforts of many secularists are often aided unknowingly by Christians themselves. Whether intimidated by opposition or misguided by a faulty understanding of their Christian mission, many live in *self-imposed* silence. Too many Christians have ignored the mandate to manifest God's truths in all areas of our culture.

Unfortunately, many Christians have fallen prey to the ruse that religion is a personal matter—"personal" meaning that one may express it at home or in church, but had better keep it out of the public arena. Thus, many have segregated their lives into the "spiritual" and the "secular." Family devotions, evangelism, Bible study, Sunday church services and the like fall into the spiritual compartment; every other area—business, education, politics, etc.—is strictly secular. As a result, Christians have "privatized" their faith, and have withdrawn their influence from politics, education and other vital areas of public life.

This retreat from society has left the field open for the unopposed influx of secularistic thought that is now entrenched as the dominant force in American society. As a consequence, America is saturated with a system of arbitrary absolutes and philosophical relatives that have man at their center. Even now, with many of our once-sturdy foundations crumbling around us—economically, politically, academically, morally—the *potency* of the Christian voice has yet to be raised effectively.

We must recognize that Christ came to redeem the *whole* man, and He is to be Lord of the Christian's *whole* life. As such, we are to integrate God's teachings into every area of our lives. There should be no differentiation between the "spiritual" and the "secular." No compartment is outside the jurisdiction of Christ's lordship.

Recognizing Christ's absolute and all-encompassing lordship—not only in our individual lives, but in all areas of our lives—should move us to fulfill His commission to make His teachings known in all of life's areas. This is the true meaning of evangelism.

Jesus has also called us to be "salt" and "light"—to redeem our *present* world through the integration of God's truth. This is a mission many have sorely neglected. Instead of seeking to externalize the gospel and make its application relevant to the world around us, many have hid their lights under a basket and shelved the Christian salt until it has lost most of its flavor.

But the consequences are *not* irreversible.

The solution to the humanistic crisis in America is for Christians to end their silence and passivity and *activate* their convictions. We must boldly seek to express God's truth as it related to every area of our society, and we must defend against every effort to repress such expression.

> Many of Those Who Head the Modern Technological Elite Openly Attack the Christian Base.

137

We must remember that the great social reforms in earlier centuries were largely the result of religious revivals. These revivals were aimed not merely at "saving souls" but also at redeeming man's social environment. Simply put, early Christianity saw God at work in the whole culture, not merely in the hearts of men.

This attitude motivated many Christians to fight doggedly for the abolition of slavery and other social reforms that testified to God's view of the dignity of man. These Christians were determined to apply the principles of their faith to the practical needs of their cultures. This faith and determination resulted in significant social improvements as well as in personal conversions.

There is no reason to doubt that similar reforms are possible today. We have access to the limitless power of God. We also have the foundation to our nation's Christian heritage, as reflected in our Declaration of Independence and the United States Constitution.

Christians should keep in mind that when it comes to expressing our convictions, the Constitution—according to the original intent of its framers—*is on our side.* Regardless of how others may invoke the First Amendment to restrict and subdue religious influence, the Supreme Court has affirmed that the Constitution's intent is *not* to expunge religion from all public society. Rather, the First Amendment dictates that the government must protect and accommodate religion, not be hostile to it. Thus, we have a constitutional foundation for protecting outright efforts to censor our convictions, since these indeed show hostility toward religion.

It is imperative that the right of Christians to express themselves be carried into all public arenas (or our freedom to speak at all may be lost). This includes the public schools. Studies by youth organizations have shown that if a person does not trust in Christ by the time he is 18, the odds are high that he *never* will. Therefore, if Christians give in to secularistic attacks and relinquish their rights to voice their convictions, then we may totally *lose* the opportunity to reach a vast segment of society with the truth of the Gospel.

We must also protect the rights of religious parents to direct their children's education free from excessive government interference. The Bible states that parents are responsible for the education of their children, and allowing state encroachment on that responsibility is a threat to family strength and liberty.

Most important of all, we must boldly speak out against the horrors of abortion, aggressively defending the rights of the unborn child. Within the abortion issue lies the total destruction of freedom as we know it. A government that will not protect human life will not, in the end, protect any freedoms or liberties.

Putting Faith to the Test.

Such efforts, however, will be accompanied by risk. In the examples mentioned at the beginning of this article, there was considerable risk to the comfort and well-being of the people involved. Nevertheless, they stood the ground of their convictions, refusing to back down even when threatened with financial penalty or prison terms. In most cases, their faith and determination brought about favorable change.

For example:

In the midst of legal delays and litigation that lasted nearly two years, David and James Henderson continued to picket the abortion clinic, protesting what they termed the "horrendous and butcheristic slaughter of unborn human children." The threat of a $200,000 lawsuit was not enough to deter them.

The Hendersons' willingness to choose the *right* action over the safe or convenient action led to positive results. On several occasions, women decided not to go through with the abortion they had planned to have that day, and one source of statistics indicated that the clinic performed 100 fewer abortions in 1983, compared with previous years. Furthermore, a Superior Court judge *upheld* the brothers' constitutional rights to freedom of speech, and dismissed all charges of libel and defamation.

In the case of the Roman Catholic nurse who refused to work for an abortionist, when the state disqualified her from receiving unemployment compensation, she didn't passively submit. She sought the help of Christian attorneys, who threatened to sue the state for violating her constitutional rights. At that point the *state* backed down and restored her benefits.

In the home education case, when Terry and Vickie Roemhild were found guilty of violating Georgia's compulsory education statute, they didn't acquiesce when faced with a heavy fine. They appealed the decision to a higher *court,* defending their parental responsibility to give their children good academic and moral instruction—both of which they found lacking in the public schools. The Georgia Supreme Court ruled that the compulsory education statute was "impermissibly vague" and therefore unconstitutional—thus upholding the right of the couple to teach their children at home. In effect, the state learned that it does not have the license to regulate through *arbitrary interpretations* of the law.

Conclusion.

When the apostle Peter was ordered to stop preaching and teaching about Jesus, he refused, saying, "We must obey God rather than men" (Acts 5:29). Peter was jailed, beaten and finally executed for his commitment to spreading the truth of the Gospel. To him—and to the first-century Christians—faith was not a "personal" matter, something to be quietly confined to church and home. It was God's universal truth given to redeem a crumbling world.

We must be diligent in ensuring that Christianity is given an *equal* voice in the marketplace of ideas. It will not be easy. The closed system of secularism will logically attempt to exclude any mention of Christianity, except to mock it. However, if Christians will consistently, and without hesitation, proclaim their ideas in all areas of the culture, they can be confident that the truth of Christianity will prevail in a truly *open* marketplace of ideas.

GOD'S JUDGMENT ON NATIONS

The foundations of present day America are no longer solid rocks cemented in its Christian heritage: They have become brittle clay crumbling under the judgment of God.

The landscape of history is strewn with the remains of nations, once great, who let moral decay from within bring them to ruin.

As the Roman Empire rose to greatness, its populace no doubt assumed that it would be around for centuries to come. But even while its citizens romped in apparent prosperity, its foundations were crumbling underneath them. And so historians record "The Rise and the Fall of the Roman Empire."

Greece gave the world its first historical attempt at democracy, splendid architecture, excellence in culture. It produced a dazzling roster of men, including Socrates, Plato and Aristotle. Greek civilization rose to its "Golden Age," until corruption set in: in politics, business, personal life, even religion. According to a popular proverb, there were more gods in Athens than men! The apostle Paul clearly identified that nation's spiritual poverty when from Mars Hill he preached his famous sermon on their "unknown God." In time Greece fell. And with it their democracy fell, because Greece did not have the moral fiber to undergird it.

Other great civilizations have come and gone. The ancient Mayan nation developed brain surgery, excelled in mathematics and astronomy, and built an incredible network of irrigation canals. Then corruption took hold. Today it is a ghost of the past.

America: Next on the List?

Is God blind to the sin of our own nation? Will He continue to bless us as He looks on our idols of silver and gold, on our pride of personal achievement, on our prevailing rebellion against Him?

The Bible repeatedly warns that, without repentance, judgment is inevitable. "Righteousness exalteth a nation; but sin is a reproach to any people."

America is not big enough to shake her fist in the face of a holy God and get away with it.

Does the black shadow of judgment already loom over our land?

As America has permitted homosexuality to establish itself as an "alternate lifestyle," it has also reeled from the frightening spread of sexually transmitted diseases. Sin begets its own consequences, both on individuals and nations.

As it opened the doors to abortion, it found itself a party to wholesale murder and inherited a whole new set of social problems.

As it pulled the Judeo-Christian moral foundations from its schools, it invited an epidemic of drugs, rebellion and classroom assaults.

As it let its military respect slide, the Communists added new pieces of geography to its campaign of world conquest, and millions more around the world lost their freedoms.

While the economy has seemingly rebounded, at least for the moment, some analysts still point to the darkening shadows of economic catastrophe.

Stories of crime, corruption and sex scandal fill the newspapers. Conservatives and liberals alike agree that our beloved nation has some gaping wounds. Sadly, though, the combined attempts of analysts, politicians, educators and sociologists are failing miserably to provide any lasting solutions.

Why?

We have failed to understand the *cause* of our problems. As a result, we are merely treating symptoms, while ignoring the real *roots*.

The Root of the Problem.

Sociologists worry about the escalating illegitimate birth rate and the alarming spread of venereal diseases. Scientists and doctors search for cures and for more effective means of birth control. Yet at the *root* of both these

problems is sexual promiscuity. In public discussions of these subjects, seldom is chastity proposed as a solution. Man wants to live without restraints, but also avoid the consequences. It simply is not possible.

The American public expresses its outrage at the growing problem of child abuse and sexual molestation. But is such behavior really very surprising in a sex-crazed society that exalts moral perversion on television, in movies and magazines, and when pornography is pumped wholesale into the living rooms of America?

The sin of a self-centered lifestyle comes back on both individuals and society.

The Scriptures declare that God will send confusion, rebuke, even ruin, upon the nation that forsakes Him. "All the nations will ask, 'Why has the Lord done this to the land?' And the answer will be, 'It is because this people abandoned the covenant of the Lord, the God of their fathers.' "

Civilizations do not just die. Their leaders and people are first deceived; then they are destroyed by God.

"Let no man deceive you with vain words: for because of these things (immorality, covetousness, worship of false gods, etc.) cometh the wrath of God upon the children of disobedience (Eph. 5:6).

The deception comes in the form of "the lie": "...God shall send them strong delusion, that they should believe the lie" (II Thess. 2:11).

"The lie" was first given to Eve in the

> America Is Not Big Enough to Shake Her Fist in the Face of a Holy God and Get Away with It.

142

garden of Eden: "...ye shall be as gods, knowing (deciding for yourselves) good and evil" (Gen. 3:5).

When a Nation Listens to "The Lie"...

It dethrones God and deifies man's achievements.

It exalts human reason as supreme.

It trusts education and science to solve its problems.

It believes that man is evolving into perfection.

It replaces God's moral standards with situational ethics.

It promotes sensual pleasure and instant gratification.

It strives for a world utopia of prosperity and peace.

It makes the State the sovereign dictator over everyone.

WHY DID THE ROMAN EMPIRE FALL?

The events which led to the collapse of the Roman Empire are startlingly similar to the events which are occurring in our nation today.

Historical Sequence.

1. *Strong Families:* Rome was founded on high moral standards. Each father was respected as the head of the family. In the early republic, the father had legal authority to discipline rebellious members of his family.

2. *Home Education:* The education of the children was the responsibility of the parents. This further strengthened the children's honor and respect for their parents and also deepened the communication and understanding between parents and children.

3. *Prosperity:* Strong Roman families produced a strong nation. The Roman armies were victorious in war. The wealth of conquered nations increased Roman prosperity and prestige.

4. *National Achievements:* Great building programs began in Rome. A vast network of roads united the empire. Magnificent palaces, public buildings, and coliseums were constructed.

5. *Infiltration of "The Lie":* As Roman families prospered, it became fashionable to hire educated Greeks to care for the children. Greek philosophy, with its humanistic and godless base, was soon passed on to the Roman families. Women demanded more rights and, in order to accommodate them, new marriage contracts were designed, including "open marriages."

6. *Big Government:* By the first century A.D. the father had lost his legal authority. It was delegated to the village, then to the city, then to the state, and finally to the empire. In Rome, citizens complained about housing shortages, soaring rents, congested traffic, polluted air, crime in the streets, and the high cost of living.

Unemployment was a perennial problem. To solve it, the government created a multitude of civil service jobs, including building inspectors, health inspectors, and tax collectors.

7. *Decline and Persecution:* The problem of big government only multiplied. Meanwhile, a flourishing New Testament Church was established in the Roman Empire through the preaching of the Apostle Paul and others. The final act of the Roman Empire was to bring great persecution to these Christians.

Rome was quite tolerant of all religions except Christianity. Christianity was banned and Christians were persecuted, burned, and thrown to the lions. Why? Because the very nature of Christianity is intolerant of "the lie" of Satan which is the basis of every other religion.

By the third century, Christianity conquered pagan Rome.

THE RUINS OF GREECE

A civilization which rejected God and worshiped the human mind and body.

The basic philosophy of Greece was, "Man is the measure of all things. Man, not the gods, the relative, not the absolute."

The Greeks were committed to building the ideal society. Their three commandments were, "Honor the gods, help your friends, and adorn your city."

Only the strong survived in Greece. Deformed or weak children were hurled from cliffs or abandoned by their fathers to die. Seven-year-old boys were sent off to learn war. The human body was idolized. A man who could not swim or wrestle was scorned.

As immorality increased, the human mind became supreme. Reason itself was worshipped. The Greeks' search for knowledge was unending. Their probing produced a pantheon of skeptics, cynics, stoics, and epicureans. Greek scholars laid the foundations for the study of biology, physiology, and anatomy. Their attempt to integrate bodily ills and the psyche was the beginning of psychiatry. Athenians also had tax-financed medicare.

Soon the government became a bureaucracy bound in red tape and taxation. At one time there were 218 taxes. There was even a tax on tax receipts.

God's judgment came upon the Greek civilization according to the promise of His Word. "The wicked shall be turned into hell, and all the nations that forget God" (Psalm 9:17).

Greek ruins

A NATION ADRIFT:
A Conclusion.

I n April, 1912, the largest and most luxurious vessel ever built set forth on its maiden voyage. The British liner *Titanic* had a double-bottomed hull, divided into sixteen watertight compartments. Because as many as four of these could be completely flooded without endangering the ship's buoyancy, the *Titanic* was considered unsinkable.

On the fateful night of April 14, shortly before midnight, the great liner was steaming through the foggy North Atlantic when it collided with an enormous iceberg. A 300-foot gash was ripped in the ship's right side, rupturing five of its watertight compartments. The *Titanic* sank into the icy depths, claiming over 1,500 lives.

A tragic, though often untold story about that night concerns one man on another ship, less than 20 miles away from the *Titanic*. The other vessel was the *Californian*, and it could have come to the rescue of the sinking liner, if only someone had been listening. But the radio operator had fallen asleep on duty! When help did finally reach the disaster area it was too late to save more than a few.

The very greatness of the *Titanic* had caused her crew and passengers to feel inordinately confident. "Unsinkable" was such an assuring term. But it proved a fatal misjudgment.

Like the *Titanic*, our great ship of state, America, has gone adrift and is headed for a potentially fatal collision. Many feel she, too, is unsinkable; but that assessment is rooted in feeling, not fact. The truth of the matter is that America has already run into some "icebergs" that have damaged her hull and caused not a few leaks. She is in grave danger.

Fortunately, others are watching and listening. Unlike the sleeping radio operator, concerned friends are alert to the danger. Men like Alexander Solzhenitzyn, who has spoken so eloquently in calling America to wake up and watch out. The message is clear: It isn't too late...yet.

146

AMERICA TOMORROW:

A NATION REBORN

The hour is late; God's judgment has already begun to fall. Western civilization as we know it, is clinging precariously to the thin strand of human effort and achievement. All of man's combined attempts, time, wealth, and ability alone are not adequate to hold back the destruction of our nation. We are engaged in a great spiritual battle between the very forces of Heaven and Hell. Human weapons will not suffice. Only divine intervention will return this nation to solid footing.

Yet there is hope—hope as great as the goodness and grace of God! The sovereign ruler of the universe stands eager to manifest Himself to a generation that has never clearly seen God. He is ready to extend His mercy on our behalf.

All the resources of God Almighty are at our disposal! He rules in all the affairs of men. "He turns the king's heart whithersoever He will." Nothing is too hard for God. There is no disease He cannot heal; no condition He cannot change. God wants to come and bless our land today. He wants to heal us and forgive our sins. He wants to raise high in our nation the standard of His holiness.

But if judgment is to be averted, we must meet God's conditions. Four thousand years ago, when Israel was an infant nation, God knew that they would eventually sin and experience His consequent judgment. Thinking of the time when Israel would be at the end of her resources and in a hopeless condition, God made a wonderful promise: "If My people which are called by My name will humble themselves and pray and seek My face and turn from their wicked ways, then will I hear from Heaven and will forgive their sin and heal their land" (II Chron. 7:14).

If there was ever a time when we as a people needed to seek God and cry out to Him for mercy, it is now. Now is the time for us to turn to Him, commit our lives wholeheartedly to Him, and cooperate with Him in rebuilding the spiritual foundations that have been destroyed.

The pain that our nation now feels does not have to be the agonizing pain of death. Rather it can be—it must be—the rejoicing pain of birth—the rebirth of our nation.

Indeed, I tremble for my country when I reflect that God is just, and that His justice cannot sleep forever.

THOMAS JEFFERSON

"We have been the recipients of the choicest bounties of heaven. We have been preserved, these many years, in peace and prosperity. We have grown in numbers, wealth and power, as no other nation has ever grown. But we have forgotten God. We have forgotten the gracious hand which preserved us in peace, and multiplied and enriched and strengthened us; and we have vainly imagined, in the deceitfulness of our hearts, that all these blessings were produced by some superior wisdom and virtue of our own. Intoxicated with unbroken success, we have become too self-sufficient to feel the necessity of redeeming and preserving grace, too proud to pray to the God that made us! It behooves us, then to humble ourselves before the offended Power, to confess our national sins, and to pray for clemency and forgiveness."

—*April 30, 1863*
President Abraham Lincoln's Proclamation
for a National Day of
Fasting, Humiliation and Prayer

MAY GOD HEAL OUR LAND

BY JOHN PRICE

The voice of God can be clearly heard in history.
America needs to hear that voice today.

General Lew Wallace was a scholar in his time. He served in the Civil War as a Territorial Governor, and as the Governor and U.S. Senator from Indiana.

Wallace decided to disprove what history taught concerning Jesus of Nazareth. He put his mind to the task of debunking the "Christ matter" once and for all. As a learned scholar, he anticipated no problem; it was a matter of gathering enough treatises and writings.

In setting about to change history by exposing the falsity of Christianity, General Wallace instead changed it by finding Christ. The more Wallace read, the more he was forced to accept the role of God in history. Finally, he reached the conclusion that many other critics had come to; God not only is in the history of man, he also intervened in that history with his Son, Jesus Christ.

Lew Wallace never wrote his book proving Christ false; he wrote the classic *Ben Hur, A Tale of the Christ.*

And so it must be with any man who seeks the truth, for God has so firmly placed his fingerprint on the history of mankind that no one who examines it can question that it is of God.

History: Same Song, Second Verse.

Throughout man's history, man has fulfilled the old law "that the only constant is change." Man's memory is short. The very generation which God freed from Egypt turned to grumbling within one month after their liberation. Their eyes were on the fleshpots of Egypt, rather than the Promised Land.

Dr. C.I. Scofield has illustrated man's failing in his analysis of Israel: a fourfold cycle of "rebellion, retribution, repentance and restoration." God's people, whether in the Bible or in post biblical times, have lived this cycle repeatedly. First, God blesses His believers with abundance, peace and joy. Then man soon forgets that it all came from God. Pride sets in.

From pride comes rebellion, as each new generation thinks that it is great because it is wise, and then comes sin (which each generation says is not sin "in these modern times" but instead liberation from the "overly restrictive ways of the past").

God, being long-suffering and patient, allows His people to drift away and sin because He knows what is com-

THE REBIRTH OF AMERICA

ing. Sin leads to sin and the corruption of man increases. After matters have come to an accelerated state of decay, our Lord could let it all continue to fester and grow worse; however, His love for us requires that He call us back to repentance. The call to repentance is then given prior to the third stage, retribution. History shows that the call to repentance is nearly always "preceded by a period of gross iniquity, disgrace, and consequent fear."

What Happens When a Nation Repents.

History's lessons must be considered quite seriously by American Christians who seek repentance for our land. There will be some in America who, upon hearing the increasing calls for national repentance, will dismiss any need for revival. Others may see the need, but doubt revival can happen. They will say that we live in a modern time, that America is too large and diverse to expect history to repeat itself.

God has given us the history of the great city-state of Nineveh as an example of what *can* happen to a large nation which humbles itself and repents. Or, what can happen if it doesn't.

Nineveh, the capital of mighty Assyria, was mightier than Babylon. Nineveh was located at the juncture of two rivers, and like greater New York, for example, the limits of the city extended for many miles. In fact, it required a three-day trip to circle metropolitan Nineveh. The inner city of Nineveh (comparable to the borough of Manhattan) was fortified by five walls and three moats. The major wall was fifty feet high and extended for eight miles. The wall was broad enough at the top to allow four chariots to race adjacent to each other.

Nineveh's population is not precisely known, but we know that the city had 120,000 infants; hence we can guess that Nineveh, had about one million inhabitants—substantially larger than the city of San Francisco today.

God determined that he would call Nineveh, which was not an Israelite nation, to repentance. For this job, he chose Jonah, an Israelite, one of the traditional enemies of Assyria.

"Now the word of the Lord came to Jonah...saying, 'Arise, go to Nineveh, that great city, and cry against it; for their wickedness is come up before me.' "

Jonah arose, but he didn't head for Nineveh; instead he bought passage on a boat and headed in the opposite direction. The story of Jonah and the whale is well known. God saw that Jonah landed in Nineveh, however unusual the transportation.

Reluctantly, Jonah entered Nineveh and proclaimed, "Yet forty days, and Nineveh shall be overthrown" (Jonah 3:4). To Jonah's own amazement, the people "believed God and proclaimed a fast, and put on sackcloth, from the greatest of them even to the least of them." Word reached the king, who ordered that all "cry mightily unto God; yea, let them turn every one from his evil way...Who can tell if God will turn and repent, and turn away from his fierce anger, that we perish not?"

God promptly restored a repentant nation, and granted a delay in the city's predicted destruction—in this case, 160 years. Those who repented and many of their descendants were spared the destruction that finally came in 612 B.C.

What Happens When a Nation Does Not Repent.

Later, in the Book of Nahum, we get a look at how Nineveh had retrogressed since its national repentance and before its final destruction. One commentator says that Nineveh's "surrounding nations were corrupted so that they ministered to the luxuries and vice of Nineveh. Merchants, motivated by greed for gold, sold their wares in a city lusting for fine things. Morality and honesty were allowed to perish so that wealth may be acquired and pleasure enjoyed." The description of Nineveh could easily fit the United States today.

Nineveh was totally destroyed, and not a single person remained there. Later, when Alexander the Great came through that area, he passed by close to Nineveh without being aware that the site of Nineveh was near. In fact, for hundreds of years many thought that the Nineveh story was only a myth because, unlike other world cities, which continued to grow and expand, nobody even knew where it had been located, if in fact it ever did exist.

The site of Nineveh was discovered, though, in 1840 under thirty to forty-five feet of strata built up through the years. The site confirms all of the biblical descriptions; its walls, its size, its fine palaces, numerous written clay tablets which had been bills of sales, invoices, historical records, and literature.

Each age thinks it is in a "modern time" as it is compared to times past. One can look back and see apparent progress in the arts and sciences from any age. What we fail to see is that our moral change is sin, not progress.

The Ninevites enjoyed the best chariots, finest food, most exotic entertainment, stoutest drink, and an extensive business and commercial system like none other in the world. In addition, Assyria had ruled the known world for 200 years or so and led the world in military might. Rumors of growing Babylonian military power must have been dismissed as nonsense.

Alarmed over the state of the nation, various Christian leaders have called for the election of Christian congressmen as a solution to our troubles. Though many of our problems emanate from Washington, D.C., and though a Congress which sought to reverse America's decline could have major impact, the real question is, how many of America's problems come from the top and how many are based upon a widely spread populace who are in general agreement with current policies?

What America needs is a sweeping meaningful revival of believers who humble themselves and who bring millions more into the ranks of God's redeemed. If this nation has a real repentance at the individual level, then our leaders will reflect that basic change in America.

If we begin to see national revival sweeping America, we will begin to see Christians united in common effort to pray, drawn together by their common faith and their desire to call the nation to repentance.

Repentant Christians in prayer will be able to do more for America than all of the government programs rolled into one. They will find the purpose and power that allows them to take public stands in league with their fellow believers which could radically change the future of America.

HAVE YOU CHANGED YOUR MIND?

BY CHARLES W. COLSON

"Repent! For the Kingdom of God is at hand."

For most of us the word "repent-ance" conjures up images of medieval monks in sackcloth and ashes or Old Testament prophets rending their garments in anguish. Or we see repentance as something someone "really wicked" must do to sanitize his corrupt life.

But repentance is much more than self-flagellation, more than regret, more than deep sorrow for past sins; and it applies to everyone. The biblical word for repentance is "metanoia" in the original Greek. Meta means "change" and noia means "mind," so literally it means "a change in mind, heart, and life, wrought by the Spirit of God." [1]

Thus, repentance is replete with radical implications, for a fundamental change of mind not only turns us from the sinful past, but transforms our life, plans, values, ethics, and actions as we begin to see the world through God's eyes rather than ours. That kind of trans-formation requires the ultimate surrender of self.

Consistent Theme of the Old Testament.

The call to repentance—individual and corporate— is one of the most consistent themes of Scripture. The Old Testament contains vivid accounts of kings and prophets, priests and people falling before God to plead for mercy and promising to change. The demand for repentance is clear in God's commands to Moses (Lev. 26:40,41), and its broken-hearted reality and passion flow through David's eloquent prayer of contrition (Psalm 51). It is the consistent refrain of the prophets.

Keynote of the New Testament.

Repentance is the keynote of the New Testament as well. It is John the Baptist's single message: "Repent and believe the good news," were among Jesus' first public words. And His last instructions to His disciples before the Ascension included the directive that "repentance and forgiveness of sins will be preached in His name to all nations" (Mark 24:47). All told, the words "repent" or "repentance" appear more than fifty times in the New Testament.

Repentance is an inescapable consequence of regeneration, an indispensable part of the conversion process that takes place under the convicting power of the Holy Spirit. But repentance is also a continuing state of mind. We are warned, for example, to repent before partaking of communion. Also, believers "prove their repentance by their deeds" (Acts 26:26). Without a continuing repentant attitude— a persistent desire to turn away from our own nature and seek God's nature—Christian growth is impossible. Loving God is impossible.

Why Repentance Isn't Preached.

If all this is true, then, some may ask, why is repentance so seldom preached and so little understood? I believe there are three reasons:

Noted church historian J. Edwin Orr sums up the first: the appeal of modern evangelism is "not for repentance but for enlistment." [2]

The second reason repentance is so ignored or misunderstood comes much closer to home, as I have discovered: Often we are simply unwilling or unable to accept the reality of personal sin and therefore to accept our need for repentance.

And this leads us to the third reason for our shallow understanding of repentance: our culture has written sin out of existence. Even Christians, who should understand the basic truth that all are heirs of Adam's fall and thus all are sinners, are influenced, often blinded, by humanist values.

Humanism began in the Garden when the tempter invited Eve to be "like God." Ever since it has encouraged us to believe what our sinful nature wants us to believe—that we are good, getting better through science and education, and can through our own efforts become perfect, masters of our own fate. We can be our own god.

Whatever became of sin? Karl Menninger's startling book title and theme is the most timely question anyone could ask of the church today. The answer lies within each of us, but to find it we must come face to face with who we really are. This is a difficult process. That hidden self is buried deep inside our hearts, and as Jeremiah warned, the human heart is deceitful above all things (Jer. 17:9). Confronting that true self is an excruciating discovery.

⟡

"Sin is a deep-seated, loathsome disease that is eating the heart out of humanity and cursing, blighting, damning, wrecking, and ruining those who tamper with it."
JOE HANKINS

THEREFORE ALSO NOW, SAITH THE LORD, TURN YE EVEN TO ME WITH ALL YOUR HEART, AND WITH FASTING, AND WITH WEEPING, AND WITH MOURNING... AND TURN UNTO THE LORD YOUR GOD: FOR HE IS GRACIOUS AND MERCIFUL...

JOEL 2:12-13

ISAIAH SPEAKS TO AMERICA

BY DEL FEHSENFELD JR.

*Our Nation must heed the trumpet of the prophet of God,
or be cast down by its very sound.*

The prophet Isaiah was never voted one of the "Ten Most Popular Christian Leaders" of his day. This fervent intercessor and uncompromising prophet rarely received applause for his messages. For he spoke the truth. And the truth pierced the consciences and threatened the godless lifestyles of his hearers.

Although specifically directed at God's chosen nation of Israel, Isaiah's words are a frighteningly accurate description of America in this final quarter of the 20th Century.

As we examine the message of the ancient prophet, it becomes apparent that the shortcomings of our nation are no more than a magnified reflection of the sins of God's people. "Hear, O heavens, and give ear O earth: for the Lord hath spoken, 'I have nourished and brought up children, and they have rebelled against Me' " (Isaiah 1:2).

To the undiscerning observer, religion was flourishing in Israel, Sacrifices and incense were offered with regularity. Religious holy-days, rituals, and feasts were faithfully observed.

But under the scrutinizing eye of a holy God, the external mask of piety could not hide the underlying, ugly reality of sin, idolatry, and rebellion. The prophet became in God's hand an instrument to lift the deceptive mask.

God's grievances against His people are numerous. Perhaps they are best summarized in Chapter 5 of Isaiah's prophecy. This passage reveals not only God's case against Israel, but also the grave need of God's people today for repentance and cleansing.

The Menace of Materialism.

1. *"Woe unto them that join house to house, that lay field to field, till there be no place, that they may be placed alone in the midst of the earth!"* (Isaiah 5:8). Here was a people motivated by temporal gain and material prosperity. Never content with the provision of their basic needs, their sights were ever on the accumulation of more and better "things." It's not that "God, who giveth us richly all things to enjoy" objected to their having fine possessions. The problem was in their heart attitude. Their ultimate goal was to exist "alone in the midst of the earth"—to live for "self," to be exalted above others, to escape the burdens and cares of others, to be far away from the demands and realities of life.

As God's people living in a materialistic, greedy society, we are all too often guilty of the same attitude. Rather than seeking the eternal riches of His righteousness and giving ourselves to meet the spiritual needs of others, our energy is consumed in indulging the appetites of our flesh. We want to be left alone, to add to our grasp more houses, lands, stocks, securities, cars retirement funds, personal luxuries and conveniences.

The Pursuit of Pleasure.

2. *"Woe unto them that rise up in the morning, that they may follow strong drink; that continue until night, 'till wine inflame them! And the harp, and the viol, the tabret, and pipe, and wine, are in their feasts: but they regard not the work of the Lord, neither consider the operation of His hands"* (Isaiah 5:11,12). The hedonistic, pleasure-seeking nation of Israel did not have time to seek after God. They lived only to please themselves (Isaiah 2:6). Apparently they even entertained themselves with the sensual "pictures of desire" (Isaiah 2:16). With blithe disregard for the future, they lived only for the "here and now."

Perhaps nothing saps more vitality and power from the life of God's people today than the pursuit of pleasure. We have time for television ("pictures of desire"), ballgames, movies, parties, vacations, tennis, gold and magazines. But we can't find time to pray, to study God's Word, to disciple our children, to serve, to witness.

3. *"Woe unto them that draw iniquity with cords of vanity, and sin as it were with a cart rope"* (Isaiah 5:18).

The picture here is one of open, blatant rebellion. God's people do not even attempt to hide their sin; they have no sense of shame. How the heart of the Saviour must grieve to see His blood-bought Bride enjoying and flaunting every conceivable sin. Sin is being openly practiced and tolerated— bitterness, anger, lack of love, pornography, adultery, fornication, divorce, worldliness, and on and on.

4. *"Woe unto them that call evil good, and good evil; that put darkness for light; and light for darkness; that put bitter for sweet, and sweet for bitter!"* (Isaiah 5:20).

The Binding of Boastfulness.

Through repeated disobedience, the conscience of the nation of Israel had been seared; God's people developed a twisted, perverted sense of right and wrong. They could no longer discern between good and evil. They indulged and found satisfaction in the things God hates. They scoffed at the values of God.

No one can argue that our nation has adopted values and standards contrary to those of God. "Hands that shed innocent blood" are an abomination to God. Yet our courts protect the "right" of a mother to take the life of her unborn child. God resists the proud heart. But our society encourages ladder climbing, self-assertion, and the independent, self-sufficient spirit. God's design for the family calls for submission and yielding of rights. Our system demands equal

> # The Short-comings of Our Nation Are No More Than a Magnified Reflection of the Sins of God's People.

THE REBIRTH OF AMERICA

rights for all. God created the man to provide leadership and the woman to respond to his leadership with a gentle, quiet spirit. In our world, the assertive women receives the applause, and men have defaulted their responsibility to lead.

5. "Woe unto them that are wise in their own eyes, and prudent in their own sight!" (Isaiah 5:21). In their pride and arrogance, the Israelites had become blinded to their true spiritual condition. They had an inflated view of themselves. They could not see the foolishness of their own so-called "wisdom."

How like so many of us as believers. We have the answer to everything. Just ask us! Our shelves are filled with notebooks on everything. The only problem is we haven't learned how to live—how to have a holy, humble relationship with God and with others.

We are too proud to admit our real spiritual needs. We don't want anyone to think that our marriage is struggling, that our children are rebellious, that our walk with God is shallow and frustrating, or that we can't control our angry, impatient, and critical responses.

Isaiah's Indictment of Israel.

6. "Woe unto them...which justify the wicked for reward, and take away the righteousness of the righteous from him!" (Isaiah 5:23).

Perverted justice is a characteristic of a society that has forsaken God. Motivated by greed and personal gain, cor-ruption becomes an accepted way of life.

The Wages of Sin.

Written into the constitution of God's universe are certain consequences for sin. And Israel was not exempt. In the early chapters of his prophecy, Isaiah graphically describes the price Israel had to pay for her disobedience.

Her country was desolate and her cities were burned with fire (1:7). The land was overthrown by strangers (1:7). Their sacrifices were unacceptable to God and of no value (1:11). God refused to hear or answer their prayers (1:15). God forsook those who had forsaken Him (2:6). God took away their food and other basic provisions (3:1). There was a dearth of "mighty men" to provide spiritual, political, and social leadership (3:4). Social oppression was great (3:5). Young people were arrogant and had no respect for authority (3:5). Ultimately, they were taken into captivity and chastised by God, that they might learn obedience, dependence, and humility.

> **Written into the Constitution of God's Universe Are Certain Consequences for Sin.**

God's Offer of Mercy to Israel ...and America.

In spite of the hardened, idolatrous ways of His people, God revealed Himself not only as a just and, vengeful God, but also as a merciful, long-suffering God of covenant love. With eyes of faith, Isaiah saw a Saviour who would one day take on Himself the full fury and wrath

163

THE REBIRTH OF AMERICA

of a holy God against sin.

Mercy was abundant and available, if God's people would only meet His conditions.

1. Return to God's Word. "Hear the word of the Lord...give ear unto the law of our God" (Isaiah 1:10).

2. Repent. "Wash you, make you clean: put away the evil of your doings from before my eyes; cease to do evil" (Isaiah 1:1).

3. Restore God as King and His righteousness as the standard for living. "Come ye, and let us walk in the light of the Lord...learn to do well; seek judgment, relieve the oppressed...If ye be willing and obedient, ye shall eat the good of the land" (Isaiah 2:5; 1:7,19).

Israel received the glorious promise that God would restore His presence and His glory in "every dwelling place" and in the "assemblies" of His cleansed people (Isaiah 4:5). He assured them that He would be for them a place of refuge, protection, and security (Isaiah 4:6).

The same God who offered healing and forgiveness to stubborn, rebellious Israel, stands waiting to send "times of refreshing" to our land. There is hope as great and limitless as God Himself. The homes and churches of our land will experience a great release of His power and purity as God's people humbly agree with Him about their need, seek His mercy, and return to Him with all their hearts.

❧

O my God, I am ashamed and blush to lift up my face to thee, my God: for our iniquities are increased over our head, and our trespass is grown up unto the heavens.

EZRA 9:6

He that covereth his sins shall not prosper: but whoso confesseth and forsaketh them shall have mercy.

PROVERBS 28:13

WASH YOU, MAKE YOU CLEAN, PUT AWAY THE EVIL OF YOUR DOINGS FROM BEFORE MINE EYES, CEASE TO DO EVIL; LEARN TO DO WELL; SEEK JUDGMENT, RELIEVE THE OPPRESSED, JUDGE THE FATHERLESS, PLEAD FOR THE WIDOW. COME NOW, AND LET US REASON TOGETHER, SAITH THE LORD: THOUGH YOUR SINS BE AS SCARLET, THEY SHALL BE AS WHITE AS SNOW; THOUGH THEY BE RED LIKE CRIMSON, THEY SHALL BE AS WOOL.

ISAIAH 1:16-18

REPENTANCE: WHO NEEDS IT?

Let us lead by example, and cleanse the house of God.

Certainly most of us are not guilty of the sins that seem to be destroying the foundations of our nation: abortion, homosexuality, pornography, government corruption, etc. Of what do we need to repent?

Failure to be Salty.

We must repent that *we have not fulfilled our function as the "salt of the earth."* Consider the properties of salt and compare the influence of God's people in our nation. Salt is used to season food. Christians ought to be the moral conscience of the nation, so that in every aspect of life, whether social, political, economic, educational, or religious, there should be the "savor" of God's ways. When used on grapefruit, salt sweetens. Christians should sweeten the bitterness of those who rebel against God. Salt is used to slay weeds that have grown up in the cracks of the pavement. Wrongdoing should be slain in our nation by the influence of God's people. Salt is used on ice to soften it. We should have a "melting" result on the hearts in our nation that are hardened against God's truth. And salt saves or preserves food from rotting. Christians should have a preserving influence on our nation, holding it back from moral spoilage and decay.

Tragically, as we have stayed in our "salt shakers," we have lost our savor and become so much like the world around us that we have become good for nothing. As a result of our failure, our nation has developed a distorted view of God. Our people have no fear of God; rather, they scorn and mock His commands and make themselves to be God.

We must repent of our failure to be salt to this generation. And we must repent for *neglecting to speak out for God.* We all stand guilty under the indictment of God who says, "When I say unto the wicked, Thou shalt surely die; and thou givest him not warning, nor speakest to warn the wicked from his wicked way, to save his life, the same wicked man shall die in his iniquity; but his blood will I require at thine hand" (Ezekiel 3:18).

Failure to Judge Personal Sin.

We must repent for judging the wickedness of our nation, while *ignoring the sin in our own homes.* Where are the virtuous women adorned with meek and quiet spirits, and living in subjection to their husbands? Where are the children who honor and obey their parents? And where are the men who can say with David, "I will walk within my house with a perfect heart. I will set no wicked thing before mine eyes" (Psalm 101:2,3).

May God forgive us, we who are called by His name, for tolerating in our own lives and homes books, magazines, television programs, and people that are not holy, pure and undefiled.

We need to turn from our wicked ways in our churches. For we have substituted playing for praying, feasting for fasting, religion for righteousness, organizing for agonizing, and compatibility for confrontation.

God's Call to Repentance.

Dear child of God, the sovereign Ruler of the universe stands eager to manifest Himself to a generation that has never clearly seen God. He is ready to extend His mercy on our behalf. Read His promise: "At what instant I shall speak concerning a nation, and concerning a kingdom, to pluck up, and to pull down, and to destroy it; if that nation, against whom I have pronounced, turn from their evil, I will repent of the evil that I thought to do unto them" (Jer. 18:7,8).

The hour is late. God's judgment has already begun to fall, but perhaps, like Sodom and Gomorrah, God would be willing to spare our nation if just a few righteous could be found. Perhaps, as in the days of Nineveh's sin, He is waiting for a man to become obedient and willing to proclaim His message to our wicked nation.

One thing is certain. God will not restrain His judgment forever. We must act now by repenting before God, pleading with Him to reestablish His priorities in our homes, churches, and nation. We must cleanse our hearts and our homes, bringing them into total conformity to His holiness.

"Therefore also now, saith the LORD, turn ye even to me with all your heart, and with weeping, and with mourning: And rend your heart, and not your garments, and turn unto the LORD your God: for He is gracious and merciful, slow to anger, and of great kindness, and repenteth him of the evil. Who knoweth if He will return and repent, and leave a blessing behind him..." (Joel 2:12-14).

❧❧❧

Repentance, to be of any avail, must work a change of heart and conduct.
THEODORE LEDYARD CUYLER

PREPARING FOR PERSONAL REVIVAL

This is the moment for self-examination.
Without it we are wasting our time with God.

God is eager to manifest His reviving presence and power in every generation. But we must take steps to prepare for the release of His fulness in our midst.

On the eve of their passage over Jordan into the Promised Land, Joshua charged the children of Israel to prepare their hearts: "...Sanctify yourselves: for tomorrow the Lord will do wonders among you" (Joshua 3:5).

The psalmist understood the importance of spiritual preparation for revival: "Righteousness shall go before Him and shall set us in the way of His steps" (Psalm 85:13).

The questions that follow are designed to reveal specific areas of spiritual need in our lives. These areas must be dealt with in preparation for personal and corporate revival.

Steps of Action

1. *Pray* the prayer of the psalmist: "Search me, O God, and know my heart: try me, and know my thoughts: and see if there be any wicked way in me, and lead me in the way everlasting" (Psalm 139:23,24).

2. *Be totally honest* as you answer each question.

3. *Agree with God* about each need He reveals in your life. Confess each sin, with the willingness to make it right and forsake it.

4. *Praise God* for cleansing and forgiveness.

5. *Renew* your mind and *rebuild* your life through meditation and practical application of the Word of God.

6. *Review* these questions periodically to remain sensitive to your need for ongoing revival.

Genuine Salvation (II Corinthians 5:17) a. Was there ever a time in my life that I genuinely repented of my sin? b. Was there ever a time in my life that I placed all my trust in Jesus Christ alone to save me? c. Was there ever a time in my life that I completely surrendered to Jesus Christ as the Master and Lord of my life?

God's Word (Psalm 119:97; 140) a. Do I love to read and meditate on the Word of God? b. Are my personal devotions consistent and meaningful? c. Do I practically apply God's Word to my everyday life?

Humility (Isaiah 57:15) a. Am I quick to recognize and agree with God in confession when I have sinned? b. Am I quick to admit to others when I am wrong? c. Do I rejoice when others are praised and recognized and my accomplishments go unnoticed by men? d. Do I esteem all others as better than myself?

Obedience (Hebrews 13:17; I Samuel 15:22) a. Do I consistently obey what I know God wants me to do? b. Do I consistently obey the human authorities God has placed over my life?

Pure Heart (I John 1:9) a. Do I confess my sin by name? b. Do I keep "short sin accounts" with God (confess and forsake as He convicts)? c. Am I willing to give up all sin for God?

Clear Conscience (Acts 24:16) a. Do I consistently seek forgiveness from those I wrong or offend? b. Is my conscience clear with every man? (Can I honestly say, "There is no one I have ever wronged or offended in any way and not gone back to them and sought their forgiveness and made it right"?)

Priorities (Matthew 6:33) a. Does my schedule reveal that God is first in my life? b. Does my checkbook reveal that God is first in my life? c. Next to my relationship with God, is my relationship with my family my highest priority?

Values (Colossians 3:12) a. Do I love what God loves and hate what God hates? b. Do I value highly the things that please God (e.g., giving, witnessing to lost souls, studying His Word, prayer)? c. Are my affections and goals fixed on eternal values?

Sacrifice (Philippians 3:7,8) a. Am I willing to sacrifice whatever is necessary to see God move in my life and church (time, convenience, comfort, reputation, pleasure, etc.)? b. Is my life characterized by genuine sacrifice for the cause of Christ?

Spirit Control (Galatians 5:22-25; Ephesians 5:18-21) a. Am I allowing Jesus to be Lord of every area of my life?

b. Am I allowing the Holy Spirit to "fill" (control) my life each day? c. Is there consistent evidence of the "fruit of the Spirit" being produced in my life?

"First Love" (Philippians 1:21,23) a. Am I as much in love with Jesus as I have ever been? b. Am I thrilled with Jesus, filled with His joy and peace, making Him the continual object of my love?

Motives (Acts 5:29; Matthew 10:28) a. Am I more concerned about what God thinks about my life than about what others think? b. Would I pray, read my Bible, give, and serve as much if nobody but God ever noticed? c. Am I more concerned about pleasing God than I am about being accepted and appreciated by men?

Moral Purity (Ephesians 5:3,4) a. Do I keep my mind free from books, magazines, or entertainment that could stimulate fantasizing or thoughts that are not morally pure? b. Are my conversation and behavior pure and above reproach?

Forgiveness (Colossians 3:12,13) a. Do I seek to resolve conflicts in relationships as soon as possible? b. Am I quick to forgive those who wrong me or hurt me?

Sensitivity (Matthew 5:23,24) a. Am I sensitive to the conviction and promptings of God's Spirit? b. Am I quick to respond in humility and obedience to the conviction and promptings of God's Spirit?

Evangelism (Romans 9:3; Luke 24:46,48) a. Do I have a burden for lost souls? b. Do I consistently witness for Christ?

Prayer (I Timothy 2:1) a. Am I faithful in praying for the needs of others? b. Do I pray specifically, fervently, and faithfully for revival in my life, my church, and our nation?

LET US SEARCH AND TRY OUR WAYS, AND TURN AGAIN TO THE LORD.

LAMENTATIONS 3:40

HOW TO BE SURE

BY ARTHUR S. DE MOSS

*The transformation of a nation begins on a personal level.
There are millions of Americans who are religious but have
never experienced a personal relationship with God.*

There's probably more uncertainty about the most important matter in the world than about any other. Let me illustrate: If you were to ask 100 persons at random about war, politics, or pollution, you would get a fairly definite opinion from most.

But ask the same 100 persons, "Are you a Christian?" or, "Are you going to Heaven when you die?" The vast majority would answer with varying degrees of doubt—"I don't know"..."I'm not sure"..."I'm working on it"..."I've no idea."

Most of these same persons would tell you that they believe in Jesus Christ, and that they believe in Heaven. Yet they don't know whether or not they are going to Heaven.

What, by the way, would your answer be?

Most of us know definitely whether or not we are working and whether or not we are married. Yet we do not know whether or not we have eternal life.

Most persons know where their destination is when they're traveling somewhere. Yet ask them where their final destination will be—where they will be living forever—and very few know!

I've talked with a great many persons about this matter, and I believe I now have a better understanding of the problem, and the reason for the uncertainty and doubt. See if you don't agree.

Basically, the misunderstanding revolves around what is involved in attaining eternal life and going to Heaven. If you were to ask the average person what one must do to have eternal life, he would probably answer by listing one or more of the following items:

1. Join a church.
2. Be baptized and/or confirmed.
3. Live a good life.
4. Obey the Ten Commandments.
5. Live by the Sermon on the Mount.
6. Go to church regularly.
7. Follow the teachings and example of Christ.

Now, all of these represent something that man does, or tries to do. They reflect the popular idea that eternal life in Heaven is a reward to be won.

But Jesus said:

"And this is eternal life, that they may know Thee the only true God, and Jesus Christ whom thou hast sent" (John 17:3).

The Bible further makes it clear that we cannot win or earn our way to Heaven. Eternal life is not a reward for what we have done or tried to do; it is a free gift.

". . . the free gift of God is eternal life in Christ Jesus our Lord" (Romans 6:23).

"For by grace you have been saved through faith; and that not of yourselves, it is the gift of God; not as a result of works, that no one should boast" (Ephesians 2:8,9).

So long as a person thinks that he must earn his way into the presence of God, he can never be certain that he is going to Heaven. He is generally honest or sensible enough to realize that he is not able to be good enough to measure up to God's perfect standards. And for one to say, "I know I am going to Heaven," sounds like the ultimate in pride and boasting, if Heaven is reached through good works.

The Bible teaches that we must realize that we cannot be good enough, that we cannot merit or work our way to Heaven—and that we do not need to! But we are to realize, instead, that the way to Heaven has been opened by what Jesus Christ has done for us. No matter how bad or good we may be, or think we are, any one of us can qualify.

The Bible tells us of those who "...not knowing about God's righteousness, and seeking to establish their own...did not subject themselves to the righteousness of God. For Christ is the end of the law for righteousness to everyone who believes" (Romans 10:3,4).

...The Misunderstanding Revolves Around What Is Involved in Attaining Eternal Life.

You see, God sent His Son, Jesus Christ, to pay for our sins—yours and mine—by His death on the cross. He paid for eternal life, and now He offers it to you and to me as a free gift. By simply recognizing our need for a divine Saviour, by turning from going our own way, and by accepting God's payment for our sins and our salvation, the matter of our eternal destiny is immediately resolved.

Do you have this assurance?

If not, you can right here and now. How? The Bible says, speaking of Jesus Christ:

"All things came into being through Him: and apart from Him nothing came into being...He was in the world, and the world was made through Him, and the world did not know Him. But as many as received Him, to them He gave the right to become children of God, even to those who believed in His name" (John 1:3,10,11).

Have you received Him?

How, you still ask?

Well, God likens our life to a home, with the heart as the door to the home.

In the last book of the Bible, Jesus said:

"Behold, I stand at the door and knock; if any one hears My voice and opens the door, I will come in to him" (Revelation 3:20).

Are you willing to open the door of your life, to turn from your sin, and to invite Jesus to come in and take control of your life? Are you willing to place all of your trust and confidence in Him and in His merits, rather than in your own? If so, let us suggest you complete the transaction by praying something along the following lines:

"Dear God, I know I am a sinner, and unable to save myself. But I do believe you love me, and that you sent your Son Jesus to die on the cross for my sins.

"Right here and now, Lord Jesus, I repent of my sins and I invite you to come into my heart, forgive my every sin, and grant me your gift of eternal life.

"Thank you, dear Lord, for hearing and answering my prayer, and for coming into my heart and life, as you promised you would. Amen."

❧

"These things have I written unto you that believe on the name of the Son of God, that ye may know that ye have eternal life, and that ye may believe on the name of the Son of God."

I JOHN 5:13

In the eighteenth century, a godly mother knew that her years of life were coming to an end. She taught her young son all that she knew about God and the Christian life.

When her son was seven, she died. That son soon rejected his mother's teaching. He went off to sea and eventually became the captain of a slave trading ship.

His crew became so disgusted with the depravity of his actions that one day when he fell overboard while in a drunken stupor, they rescued him by throwing a harpoon into him and pulling him back into the ship. Thereafter John Newton walked with a limp. Later he became a Christian, and every limp was a reminder of God's matchless grace to a wretched sinner. He is the composer of "Amazing Grace," as well as hundreds of other hymns.

IN EVIL LONG I TOOK DELIGHT

In evil long I took delight,
Unawed by shame or fear,
Till a new object struck my sight,
And stopp'd my wild career:
I saw One hanging on a Tree
In agonies and blood,
Who fix'd His languid eyes on me.
As near His Cross I stood.

Sure never till my latest breath,
Can I forget that look:
It seem'd to charge me with His death,
Though not a word He spoke:
My conscience felt and own'd the guilt,
And plunged me in despair:
I saw my sins His Blood had spilt,
And help'd to nail Him there.

Alas! I knew not what I did!
But now my tears are vain:
Where shall my trembling soul be hid?
For I the Lord have slain!
—A second look He gave, which said,
"I freely all forgive;
This blood is for thy ransom paid;
I die that thou may'st live."

Thus, while His death my sin displays
In all its blackest hue,
Such is the mystery of grace,
It seals my pardon too.
With pleasing grief, and mournful joy,
My spirit now is fill'd,
That I should such a life destroy,
Yet live by Him I kill'd!

JOHN NEWTON, 1725-1807

FORGIVEN

It was strangely dark. A thunderstorm was blowing up from the mountains, and the clouds hid the sun. Women took their children by the hand and hurried back to the city. People looked at the sky and worried. It was darkness you could feel. They stood blinking at flashes of lightning that looked like daggers of fire. The eyes, the faces, the fingers, the noise, everything focused on that center cross! From the crowd that circled that tree, words dipped in venom were shot at Him from snarling lips. And they said things like: "What's wrong Jesus? Can't you save yourself?" "Hey Jesus! You said you'd build the temple in three days. Well, you've got nails in your hands and you've got plenty of wood behind your back. Go on! Build us something. What's wrong? Can't you save yourself?" O, He could have saved Himself; but then He couldn't have saved anyone else. He is a King who failed in the eyes of the world, in order to succeed in the eyes of God. Those were your sins He suffered for. And He has with His own blood written across all the ledgers of heaven the one word: "FORGIVEN!"

DERRIC JOHNSON

THE INTERCESSOR

God's greatest movements in this world have been conditioned on, continued and fashioned by prayer. God has put Himself in these great movements just as men have prayed. Persistent, prevailing, conspicuous and mastering prayer has always brought God to be present.

How vast are the possibilities of prayer! How wide its reach! It lays its hand on Almighty God and moves Him to do what He would not do if prayer was not offered. Prayer is a wonderful power placed by Almighty God in the hands of His saints, which may be used to accomplish great purposes and to achieve unusual results. The only limits to prayer are the promises of God and His ability to fulfill those promises."

E.M. BOUNDS

"I have been driven many times upon my knees by the overwhelming conviction that I had nowhere else to go. My own wisdom, and that of all about me, seemed insufficient for that day."

ABRAHAM LINCOLN

"Sow to yourselves in righteousness, reap in mercy; break up your fallow ground: for it is time to seek the LORD, till he come and rain righteousness upon you."

HOSEA 10:12

"And judgment is turned away backward, and justice standeth afar off: for truth is fallen in the street, and equity cannot enter...and the Lord saw it, and it displeased Him that there was no man, and wondered that there was no intercessor..."

ISAIAH 59:14-16a

" Knowing that intercessory prayer is our mightiest weapon and the supreme call for all Christians today, I pleadingly urge our people everywhere to pray. Believing that prayer is the greatest contribution that our people can make in this critical hour, I humbly urge that we take time to pray—to really pray.

Let there be prayer at sunup, at noonday, at sundown, at midnight—all through the day. Let us all pray for our children, our youth, our aged, our pastors, our homes. Let us pray for our churches.

Let us pray for ourselves, that we may not lose the word 'concern' out of our Christian vocabulary. Let us pray for our nation. Let us pray for those who have never known Jesus Christ and redeeming love, for moral forces everywhere, for our national leaders.

Let prayer be our passion. Let prayer be our practice."

ROBERT E. LEE

PRAYER AND THE HEALING OF AMERICA

Children, equipped with the knowledge of prayer, will strike terror into the heart of evil.

I n every arena of American life God's laws are being openly, flagrantly violated. It would follow that God's wrath will not long be restrained. But God's Word says there is hope; there is a solution.

When God's People Pray...

But we must pray! We must pray humbly, acknowledging the spiritual and moral bankruptcy of our land. We must pray fervently, imploring God's cleansing and mercy. All of our combined effort, time, wealth, and ability are not adequate to hold back the destruction of our nation. We are in a great spiritual battle between the very forces of Heaven and Hell. Human weapons will not suffice. Only a mighty moving of God's Spirit will cause us to look to Him and be saved. And we must pray for this moving.

The history of ancient Israel and Judah is full of evidences that the prayers of God's people in times of crisis result in divine intervention. Remember the occasion when the powerful Moabites and Ammonites came to make war on Judah. Judah faced potential extermination. She was paying the dreadful consequences of her sin against God. Yet when King Jehoshaphat heard of the coming attack, he inquired of the Lord, he proclaimed a fast, and the people of Judah came together from every town to seek help from the Lord. King Jehoshaphat led all the men, women, and children of Judah in an earnest prayer, prevailing upon God to defend His inheritance. In humility they acknowledged that "we have no might against this great company that cometh against us; neither know we what to do: but our eyes are upon thee" (II Chron. 20:12). God heard from heaven, promised His deliverance, and won the battle in such a way that the fear of God came upon all the surrounding nations.

Without exception, when God's people united in specific prayer, God heard, answered, provided, delivered, empowered, conquered—whatever was needed!

One Person Can Make A Difference.

Often God used the prayer of one man to cause a whole nation to return to right living. When Israel returned to Jerusalem from exile, the people continued in some practices that were an abomination unto God. Ezra was appalled when he saw the sin in his nation. He tore his clothes, pulled his hair from his head and beard, and fell on his knees with his hands spread out to God and prayed. He confessed the sins of his people and pled with God for mercy. As Ezra prayed, all the people gathered around him. They made a fresh covenant with God that they would turn from their wicked ways and obey Him.

There has never been a spiritual awakening in any country or locality that did not begin in fervent prayer. Today America is in military, economic, and social trouble. We face problems so pervasive as to threaten our very survival as a free nation. But our greatest need is for a spiritual awakening. And apart from consistent, effective prayer, America will never experience the power of God in a spiritual awakening.

KEYS TO EFFECTIVE PRAYER

How can a person pray in such a way that God will be prevailed upon to heal our land?

There are conditions that must be met for a person's prayers to be effective.

Personal Salvation.

First, you must *be sure that you are a Christian.* God's promise in II Chronicles 7:14 is made to those who belong to Him ("...if my people, which are called by my name..."). Only those who have been born-again by placing their faith in Jesus Christ can effectively call upon God to bless our nation. Right now make certain that you have become a true child of God by receiving Jesus Christ as your personal Saviour.

Purity of Life.

Second, when you pray, you must *be sure that there is no unconfessed sin in your life.* The Scripture says, "If I regard iniquity in my heart, the Lord will not hear me" (Ps. 66:18). God is looking for men and women whose hearts are pure before Him. With David, ask God to search your heart. Ask Him to reveal anything in your life that offends Him. As you confess your sin, God will cleanse you and fill you with His Holy Spirit. Then you will know how to pray for things that are pleasing to Him.

Prayer According to Knowledge.

Third, in order to pray more effectively, you must *know the principles and promises of God's Word.* The Bible reveals the principles God expects all nations to obey. For example, "Thou shalt not kill." You will be able to pray more specifically for our nation when you see how we have violated God's commandments. God has also made many promises that can be claimed in prayer. Look at His promise through Jeremiah the prophet: "If at any time I announce that a nation or kingdom is to be uprooted, torn down and destroyed, and if that nation I warned repents of its evil, then I will relent and not inflict on it the disaster I had planned" (Jer. 18:7,8).

God certainly fulfilled that promise in Jonah's day. Nineveh was under God's judgment for her sin. Yet when she repented and turned from her wicked ways, God had compassion and did not bring upon her the destruction He had threatened. Let us also claim God's promises and plead with Him to turn our nation around and extend His grace on our behalf.

Prayer with Fasting.

Fourth, prayer for our nation should be accompanied by *times of fasting.* If you mean business with God, you must be willing to deny your physical desires in order to humbly and earnestly seek His face. Throughout history, God's people have fasted when in affliction, when in need of guidance, when under oppression, when struggling against the power of Satan, when seeking God's supernatural intervention, and when confessing personal or corporate sin.

Isaiah 58 describes the kind of fast that pleases God: "Is not this the fast that I have chosen? to loose the bands of wickedness, to undo the heavy burdens, and to let the oppressed go free..." (Isa. 58:6). If the bands of wickedness are to be loosed in our nation, God's people must pray and fast. Look at the result that can be expected: "And they that shall be of thee shall build the old waste places: thou shalt raise up the foundations of many generations; and thou shalt be called, the repairer of the breach, the restorer of paths to dwell in" (Isa. 58:12).

Pray in Faith.

Finally, you must *pray in faith,* believing that as Christians meet God's conditions, He will hear from heaven, forgive our sin, and heal our land. Faith pleases God. "...he that cometh to God must believe that He is, and that He is a rewarder of them that diligently seek Him" (Heb. 11:6). God reminds us through the prophet Jeremiah, "Call unto me and I will answer thee, and shew thee great and mighty things, which thou knowest not" (Jer. 33:3).

Even when all the odds seem overwhelmingly against us, even when the condition of our nation seems most desperate, we must believe that God is still the sovereign King of the universe, that He has all power and authority, and that He is compassionate, gracious, and longing to extend mercy to us.

HOW TO PRAY FOR AMERICA

*America's future depends on the prayer of its people—
we need to know how to kneel before the Lord.*

irst, confess to God the sins that our nation has committed. When Nehemiah learned of the troublesome situation Jerusalem was in, he prayed confessing "...the sins of the children of Israel, which we have sinned against thee: both I and my father's house have sinned. We have dealt very corruptly against thee, and have not kept the commandments nor the statutes, or the judgments, which thou commandest thy servant Moses" (Neh. 1:6,7).

When you pray for our nation, first ask God to forgive our national sins. Repent for the sexual perversion we have tolerated as legitimate, alternate lifestyles. Repent that the foundation of our families has been destroyed, that we no longer hold the marriage vows sacred as God does. Repent of our sin of the legalized murder of over fifteen million unborn babies, created in the image of God. Repent for allowing our children to be indoctrinated with secular humanism in the public schools. Confess to God every stand that our nation has taken contrary to His standards of right living.

Then plead with God to have mercy on our nation, to bring about a national movement of prayer, repentance, and obedience to His laws. John Wesley understood the power of prayer, to obtain God's mercy. He wrote, "Have you any days of fasting and prayer? Storm the throne of grace and persevere therein, and mercy will come down."

Remember Your Leaders: Pray for Authorities.

Second, Scripture commands us to *pray specifically for those who have authority in our nation.* Paul exhorted Timothy to pray and intercede "for kings, and for all that are in authority; that we may lead a quiet and peaceable life in all godliness and honesty" (I Tim. 2:2). He explained that if people will pray for their rulers, they will then have the freedom not only to live quiet and peaceable lives, but also to proclaim the gospel and introduce men and women to Christ.

The majority of Christians in America have neglected to exercise their right as God's children to influence by prayer the men God has allowed to bear authority. Because we have not laboured in prayer to place godly men in our government and to change the hearts of godless men who occupy office, God has allowed us to be ruled by men who are motivated by selfishness, humanistic thinking, and peer pressure.

There is another group of people who need our prayers. In this hour of crisis, we must *intercede for the men God has raised up to lead His people in the fight* against the forces of Satan in this nation. These Christian leaders are vulnerable to constant attack because of the stand they are taking for God. We need to pray that God will put a hedge of protection around them, that they will be able to discern what God wants to say, and that they will have the courage to speak God's message without ever faltering or retreating.

Pray For Those Who Are Enslaved to Sin.

Finally, we need to *pray for the millions of people in our nation who are trapped by sin.* It is easy for us to criticize the sins that are destroying our very foundation; but we must love and pray for those who are slaves to alcohol, drugs, sex, money, and self. So many people are experiencing the empty,

painful consequences of their rebellion against God. Moses stood in the gap between God and the blasphemous idolatrous, Israelites who had erected the golden calf as a monument to their independence from God. Moses interceded for the Israelites and caused God to change His mind about destroying them. Let us join this man of prayer and prevail upon God to deliver those who are shackled by the chains of sin.

Friends, America stands on the brink of disaster. Your freedoms are at stake. Your children's future is at stake. The name and character of God are at stake. "Why should the nations say, 'Where is their God?' " "As never before, we are in desperate need of the forgiving, healing hand of God. Let us join together in earnest, effective prayer that God would sweep across our sick nation with a great revival of conviction of sin and commitment of obedience.

Are you willing to bend your knees and heart and meet His conditions? Are you willing to pay the price of humility, repentance, and persistent, prevailing prayer? May God make us all willing.

❧

The spirit of man is more important than mere physical strength, and the spiritual fiber of a nation than its wealth.
DWIGHT D. EISENHOWER

THE GREATEST THING
ANYONE CAN DO FOR
GOD AND MAN IS PRAY.
IT IS NOT THE ONLY
THING, BUT IT IS THE
CHIEF THING. THE
GREAT PEOPLE OF
EARTH ARE THE PEOPLE
WHO PRAY. I DO NOT
MEAN THOSE WHO
TALK ABOUT PRAYER;
NOR THOSE WHO SAY
THEY BELIEVE IN
PRAYER; NOR YET THOSE
WHO CAN EXPLAIN
ABOUT PRAYER; BUT I
MEAN THOSE PEOPLE
WHO TAKE TIME TO PRAY.

S.D. GORDON

HOW TO INTERCEDE FOR INFLUENTIAL MEN

Everyday, men of importance make key decisions and shape the course of history: thus they call for the prayers of Americans.

Sixteen key men make daily decisions that affect the course of this nation and of your freedom. Their decisions either acknowledge God's authority, or force us to disregard His laws. These sixteen key men are the President, the two Senators from your state, the U.S. Congressman from your district, the Governor of your State, your State Senator, your State Representative, and the nine Supreme Court Justices. We have an obligation under God to intercede for these men. Think of the supernatural power of God that could be unleashed from heaven if every Christian in America would pray for these sixteen key men daily by name.

Dr. Charles Stanley, pastor of a large church in Atlanta, Georgia, has suggested ten ways to pray for these men who occupy the highest offices in the land:

1. Pray that they would realize their personal sinfulness and their daily need for cleansing of their sin by Jesus Christ.

2. Pray that they would recognize their personal inadequacy to fulfill their tasks and that they would depend upon God for knowledge, wisdom, and the courage to do what is right.

3. Pray that they would reject all counsel that violates spiritual principles, trusting God to prove them right.

4. Pray that they would resist those who would pressure them to violate their conscience.

5. Pray that they would reverse the trends of socialism and humanism in this nation, both of which deify man rather than God.

6. Pray that they would be ready to sacrifice their personal ambitions and political careers for the sake of this nation, if yielding them would be in the best interest of their country.

7. Pray that they would rely upon prayer and the Word of God as the source of their daily strength, wisdom and courage.

8. Pray they would restore dignity, honor, trustworthiness, and righteousness to the office they hold.

9. Pray that they would remember to be good examples in their conduct to the fathers, mothers, sons, and daughters of this nation.

10. Pray that they would be reminded daily that they are accountable to Almighty God for the decisions they make.

A PRAYER FOR OUR LEADERS

HEAVENLY FATHER, I thank you for our country, our Constitution, and our leaders. I pray for our President and for every elected and appointed official who serves with him.

I pray that You will build a spiritual wall of protection around the marriage and family of every national, state and local official.

I pray that You will give them the wisdom and the courage to uphold our Constitution which established a republic based on Your absolute laws, not a democracy based on the changing whims of man's reasoning.

I pray that You will rebuke Satan for the deception of his lie that we can be "as gods" in deciding for ourselves what is right and what is wrong.

O LORD, may our leaders cast down every law, policy, and personal example which weakens marriages, families, or Your moral standards.

I pray that our leaders will understand and follow the principles of Your Word. May they realize that all authority comes from You, not the voters, and that one day they will stand before You to give an account of the power You gave to them.

I base this prayer on the promise of Your Word, that if I will humble myself, pray, seek Your face, and turn from my wicked ways, then You will hear from heaven, forgive my sin, and heal my land.

In the name and through the blood of the Lord Jesus Christ, I pray,
AMEN.

THE MINISTRY OF PRAYER

The following suggestions will help you develop an effective ministry of prayer.

I. Pray.

A. Open your prayer time praising God for who He is in your life and in our nation. For example, praise Him for His mercy, without which our nation would already have been consumed in His judgment.

B. Ask God to search your heart. Confess any personal sin He reveals to you.

C. Pray for the key sixteen men in government who influence your life and our nation.

D. Seek God's direction for how you should be personally involved in turning our nation back to Him.

E. Pray about current crisis situations in our nation. Pray that God will use these to pressure us to return to humble dependence on Him.

II. Mobilize Others to Pray.

A. Find a prayer partner. Covenant together to pray daily and specifically for our nation and its leaders.

B. Open your home for prayer one night each week. Invite your friends to join you in praying for spiritual and moral awakening in our nation.

C. Encourage your pastor to set aside regular time during weekly services to pray for our nation.

PRIORITIES AND RESISTANCE

BY JOHN W. WHITEHEAD

*In order to bring about change, Christians must have
a clear plan of biblical action laid out before them.*

In Matthew 10:16 Christ sets forth the rule for Christians when they find themselves in a hostile climate. They are to be wise. Like the serpent, they must use a calm discretion in fighting for the faith.

This means Christians must be wise in their confrontations with the state. We cannot be caught fighting useless battles that get us nowhere. Time is short and resources are limited. We must use our resources in the way they count the most.

Wisdom dictates first, that resistance and civil disobedience be carried forth in a biblical manner. Second, wisdom dictates that priorities be established and followed.

Before resorting to civil disobedience, all reasonable alternatives should be exhausted. If there is an opportunity to alter the course of events through normal channels (for example, negotiation or legislation) they should be attempted.

Civil disobedience should never be perpetrated for dramatics but for its effectiveness. Throwing goat's blood on the door of an abortion clinic is dra-matic. However, it will do little to hinder the performing of abortions.

Resistance and civil disobedience are legitimate reactions to tyrannous acts of the state. Overreaction to such acts, however, can spill over into violence. That we do not want. Unmitigated violence can never be justified.

To prevent resistance or civil disobedience from degenerating into taking the law into one's hands, it should be organized and under authority. Vigilantes are not justified under Scripture.

Christians have been drawn off into many minor battles because they lack priorities. If we are to survive the coming years, it will be because Christians and others have focused on the key issues.

The key priority issues certainly include: the sanctity of human life; the protection of the traditional family; the church and the private school; and the freedom of the public arena (including public schools). This is not a checklist but a list of priorities which must be conscientiously dealt with simultaneously.

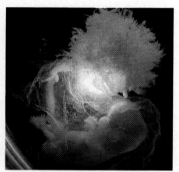

PRIORITY ONE:

The Sanctity of Human Life.

The sanctity of human life is the priority issue. It covers the entire spectrum of threats to human life including abortion, infanticide, and euthanasia. If not dealt with effectively, it spells the death of this country.

The life issue is one issue on which all Christians should be able to unite. If Christians cannot unite on this issue, then I seriously doubt there is any issue on which they can unite to bring change.

The Bible speaks strongly to our responsibility toward the spilling of innocent blood. Proverbs 24:11, 12 paraphrased, states:

Rescue those who are unjustly sentenced to death; don't stand back and let them die. Don't try to disclaim responsibility by saying you didn't know about it. For God, who knows all hearts, knows yours, and He knows you knew! And He will reward everyone according to his deeds.

If those who say they believe abortion is murder really believe it, they will do something about it. Surely if you witnessed your father, mother, brother or sister being carried into a euthanasia clinic on a stretcher you would act, and radically if necessary. The same principle applies to abortion except the child is being carried into the abortion clinic in his or her mother's womb.

Besides legislative efforts and political involvement, both of which are important, Christians can directly affect abortion in other ways. At the least, the number of babies killed can be reduced.

Churches can operate or contribute to pregnancy crisis centers. A telephone hotline can be installed and used to counsel and later to assist pregnant women.

The church should be the first place a pregnant woman comes for help. The church should assist with open homes during and after birth, until the girl is able to get on her feet.

Counselors in the church must be informed about and prepared to deal with the emotional and psychological problems faced by women who are being pressured to have abortions. These women need to know there are alternatives to abortion (such as adoption). They also need to know there is a large body of people standing by, ready to provide life-saving alternatives.

Counseling women as they enter abortion clinics and also guiding them to a local church-operated pregnancy crisis center have proved to be effective alternatives to abortion. Of course, it is vital to approach an abortion-minded woman in a compassionate and non-derogatory manner in order to be heard and to have any influence.

Picketing is another effective way to reduce the number of abortions. Some local churches use their Sunday school buses to pick up and drive their people to abortion clinics to picket.

Picketing accomplishes something other alternatives do not. In a nonviolent, lawful way it brings the issue of abortion to public light. This, coupled with the loss of business, is why abortion clinics abhor and even fight picketing.

Therefore, picketing should not be a symbolic excursion. Instead, it should be a serious attempt to close the clinic.

Picketing will definitely be resisted by the abortionist. Therefore, it must be done within legal bounds. Acquire the necessary permit from local authorities and avoid labeling abortionists, by name, as murderers or the like. Such labeling has resulted in libel and slander suits and it's not necessary.

Simply put, the church must protect those caught within the razor-like clutches of the abortionists. If not, there will be judgment and little hope for evangelism or other freedoms.

PRIORITY TWO:
The Traditional Family.

From antiquity the family has served as the basic building block of free societies. Likewise, we find a strong emphasis on the high estate of parenthood in history.

One of the few exceptions to this historical rule has been the contemporary era. Contempt of the family goes hand in hand with contempt for religion and morality. The breakdown of the faith is also the breakdown of the family.

Contempt for the family is readily illustrated by the proliferation and easy access to pornography in this country. Pornography is a very subtle attack on the family. It totally depersonalizes people. Women, especially, are portrayed more as things than as human beings.

Instead of being an expression of love, sex becomes a source of immediate gratification and eventually a form of manipulation.

The only way pornography can be curtailed is through a moral and spiritual revitilization of the people. And this will not happen until the family, the chief progenitor of morality and religion, regains its strength.

A family is built upon human relationships. It takes effort on the part of parents to develop relationships with their children. It means taking time with children, reading aloud to them, playing with them, working with them, shopping with them, and so forth. This is all relationship building.

Children are the living messages we send to a time we will not see. They are the combined images of their parents. They must, therefore, be molded with love and compassion.

Children must be guarded and protected but not shielded altogether from reality. Reality, like strong medicine though, must come in small doses. Too much too soon obliterates the distinctions between children and adults. This is particularly evident in the realm of television.

Television, besides consuming precious time, invades the privacy of the home. It almost always teaches an ethic that runs contrary to the foundation of the traditional family. It is, then, a very subtle (although sometimes overt)

attack on the family. The obvious answer is very, very selective and limited viewing. This will, of course, not prevent bad material from seeping into your children's heads. It will, however, provide you the opportunity to educate them on what to watch. This means parents, if at all possible, should watch programs with their children. If questions arise, they can then be answered.

Working on the remedies above will improve a family. However, a family will not work if it does not follow the biblical design set forth in Ephesians 5:21-25:

"Wives, submit yourselves unto your own husbands, as unto the Lord. For the husband is the head of the wife, even as Christ is the head of the church: and He is the Saviour of the body. Therefore as the church is subject unto Christ, so let the wives be to their own husbands in every thing. Husbands, love your wives, even as Christ also loved the church, and gave Himself for it."

The principles set forth here are clear. The male is to act as the leader of the family. The wife submits to this leadership, not out of fear of her husband or because she is inferior to him, but out of her respect for Christ.

"Submission," then, does not mean enslavement. It is the "yielded, intelligent, humble obedience to an ordained authority. Christ was the ultimate example of submission. Throughout His time on earth, He submitted Himself to the will of the Father." [1]

Modern men have been feminized, and modern women have been masculinized. Sexual roles have been reversed. Men must become men again and regain their leadership role in the family. The effective father is a leader, a role model.

The family is much like a classroom. The parents, as teachers, must be effective role models. A culture will mirror what is taught by the parents in the family.

The wife plays a very important part in supporting the leadership role of the husband. This is strategic because one of man's greatest needs is for respect. The way a man can be hurt the most is by being rejected publicly or privately by his wife. This, too, is part of the loving submission process. If the wife refuses to submit to her husband, their children probably will also refuse.

In addition to the husband being the leader of the family, he is also to be a compassionate lover of his wife. Ephesians 5:25 is very clear: "Husbands, love your wives, even as Christ also loved the church, and gave Himself for it." How does Christ love the church? With a sacrificial, giving, compassionate love. A husband's love for his wife should be similar.

This places the wife in a high estate. Thus, we see the practice, for example, of men opening doors for women. Such acts have roots in Christianity and, more specifically, Ephesians 5.

In addition to being the lover and the leader for his wife, the husband needs

> Children Are the Living Messages We Send to a Time We Will Not See.

to be a good father to his children. Fathers represent God. They should reflect, therefore, as closely as possible, the Creator.

The family is not going to revive overnight. It will take work. It will be painful to accomplish because so many of the familiar roots have been unplugged.

However, it must be done. And it must be based upon Christian principles, because they are the only sure foundation for life.

PRIORITY THREE:

The Church and the Private School.

The church and the private school are discussed together since they are often locked together and because they represent the last remnants of private action that operate relatively free from state involvement.

There is no question that the church is facing the threat of increasing involvement and interference of the state in her ministries. However, a note of caution is appropriate.

Although the church should fight state regulation of the church, the battles she fights must be chosen with care. In other words, the church must draw the battle lines at the most strategic places.

Drawing the line on content control and the inherent right of the church to exist is biblical. Intrusive content control by the state, in the form of approving or disapproving the content of the teaching of God's truth, is prohibited by the Bible. The apostles were forbidden to "teach in this (Christ's) name." Peter replied to the Sanhedrin, "We must obey God rather than men" (Acts 5:28,29).

State control that threatens the inherent right of the church to exist is also objectionable. This would include such things as government attempts to define what is a true church. If the state proclaims by way of government definition that a church cannot or should not legally exist, then such government actions should be resisted.

Some, however, have not been so wise to fight the battle over intrusive content control issues. They have, for example, contested in court the state's authority to require health and safety regulations in churches and Christian schools. This is a losing battle. It also expends much time and money fighting something that churches should be doing anyway (that is, having safe buildings). Thus, as a matter of tactics it is wise for churches and Christian schools not to struggle against reasonable state health and safety regulations. It is really a side issue. Lawsuits should be fought over basics and not incidentals. In light of the issues, churches should have two immediate priorities. First, they must educate their people on the issues and the proper response to the issues.

Second, the church and Christian schools must prepare for the continuing legal and legislative battles. Watchdog committees should be formed in local churches, composed of individual members, to monitor legislation affecting the exercise of the faith.

Local church associations and national church fellowships should also establish legal defense funds. Christians must be cognizant of the fact that lawsuits have high costs in time and money. A major constitutional case today will, if it is handled properly, cost many thousands of dollars. You get what you pay for, and competent legal counsel and representation will cost money.

All this translates into organized, strategic jousting while being wary of the pit.alls laid before the church. This is essential if the church is to remain free to operate without state control.

PRIORITY FOUR:

Freedom in the Public Arena.

Our secular society quite logically and consistently is trying to close the door to the freedom of religious expression in public places. This censorship is most visible in the public schools where, as of this writing, many Christian teachers and students are severely restricted in terms of free speech.

The right to exercise one's religion was once an assumed freedom in the public schools. However, because of the great exodus of Christians from the educational professions, the reins of education were grasped and have for years been controlled by secularists.

If religious people do not regain their right to free speech in the public schools and other public places, then religion will be totally privatized, much as it is in countries like the Soviet Union. There "freedom" of religion is allowed only in a controlled church.

The United States Supreme Court has upheld the right of Christians to meet and worship on university campuses. In schizophrenic fashion, however, this same right currently is denied to high school students. Thus, Christian students and teachers are not free to meet on school property on an equal basis with others. A priority here is to establish the legal precedent to allow such a freedom.

There must also be legal precedent strengthening the Christian teacher's right, at the least, to express his or her honest opinion on the Creator or Christ. This right, too, is presently in jeopardy.

If these precedents and freedoms are not forthcoming, those Christians in public education are faced with two possibilities. Either they leave the system or resist. Again, resistance and civic disobedience will result in penalties and perpetrators of such must prepare to suffer the consequences. Consequences could range from the firing of a teacher to suspension of students. These penalties should be met with lawsuits in carefully selected test cases.

Millions of children sit entombed in an educational system that, in most instances, omits any serious reference to God. These children need to hear the truth. Thus, even those Christians who disagree with public education must seek to evangelize the public schools.

We should also fight for the right of students to have voluntary prayer in public schools. It must be truly voluntary and free of coercion. For example, if students want to meet for prayer over the lunch hour or before school begins, or to read the Bible or discuss religion, this should be their right.

Make no mistake about it: enrollment may be declining in the public schools, but they will be around for some time. If the church fails to have a significant witness in public education, where most of the next generation will be trained, then the next generation will inevitably be more hostile to Christianity than this generation. That could spell disaster.

Standing Boldly.

The story of King Hezekiah illustrates very well the spirit of our age. After Isaiah had pronounced a series of devastating curses upon Hezekiah (including a foreign state's carrying away his sons and making them eunuchs, II Kings 20) Hezekiah responded by saying: "Good is the word of the Lord which thou hast spoken. And he said, Is it not good, if peace and truth be in my days?" (verse 19). In other words, as long as Hezekiah could live his own life in peace and security, he didn't really concern himself about the terror that was coming upon future generations (including his own children).

Francis A. Schaeffer has shown that ours is an age characterized by two basic values: personal peace and affluence. These result in a willingness to compromise most everything in order to keep these values intact.

Aleksandr Solzhenitsyn speaks of how the Russian people would kneel inside the door of their apartments, pressing their ears to listen when the KGB came at midnight to arrest a neighbor. He says that if all the people would have come out and driven off the officers, sheer public opinion would have demoralized the effort to subdue a free people. But their own personal peace was more important.

There is hope if Christians once again become involved in our culture and society in a meaningful way. Christians have too long been absent from involvement in the significant issues of our times.

In the context of the slide towards authoritarianism, we must, without fear, proclaim the principles of Christ. Specifically, they are: If one serves God absolutely he cannot so serve the state; and if one, being created in the image of God, loves his neighbor he will seek to serve his fellowman (Matthew 22:37-39).

Human life, the family, the church, and our freedoms are sacred. They are endowed by God. Even the state must be made to realize this.

If the state refuses, then Christians must put their faith to the test and stand and protest invasions of our sacred freedoms. A real faith results in works. And we who perceive the very real threat in the present situation must work diligently and quickly if we are to be the witnesses Christ has commanded us to be.

THE CHOICE BEFORE US
IS PLAIN, CHRIST OR
CHAOS, CONVICTION OR
COMPROMISE, DISCIPLINE
OR DISINTEGRATION.
I AM RATHER TIRED
OF HEARING ABOUT
OUR RIGHTS AND
PRIVILEGES AS AMERICAN
CITIZENS. THE TIME IS
COME, IT NOW IS, WHEN
WE OUGHT TO HEAR
ABOUT THE DUTIES AND
RESPONSIBILITIES OF OUR
CITIZENSHIP. AMERICA'S
FUTURE DEPENDS UPON
HER ACCEPTING AND
DEMONSTRATING GOD'S
GOVERNMENT.

PETER MARSHALL

"... And That Government of the People, by the People, for the People Shall Not Perish From the Earth."

THE BASIS FOR POLITICAL INVOLVEMENT

*The political process was made for man,
not man for the political process.*

For thirty years, the Bible-believing Christians of America have been largely absent from the executive, legislative, and judicial branches of both federal and local government. Many special-interest groups, promoting their cause, have successfully lobbied for and against legislation. But increasing amounts of legislation endorsing various forms of immorality, and attacking the freedoms of the church and the traditional, monogamous family, indicate that believers have not been on the scene to prevent the enactment of such legislation. After all, many well-meaning Christians insist the sole function of the people of God is to concentrate on "spiritual" matters. Let matters of civil authority be handled by others.

The Bible has much to say concerning the influence that God's people ought to have on the world in which we live.

The Call to be Light.

Jesus described Christians as the light of the world. "Let your light so shine before men, that they may see your good works, and glorify your Father which is in heaven" (Matt. 5:16). In the last two decades, Christians have begun to take that mandate seriously. As never before, through books, music, mass media, and personal witnessing, the church has become a visible light before lost men.

The Call to be Salt.

But Jesus also likened His people to the salt of the earth. The educational, political, economic and social institutions of the United States are in desperate need of salting. As salt, we need to create in these institutions a thirst for Jehovah God. We can be used of God as a moral and spiritual preservative in our nation!

Scriptural Examples of Political Involvement.

Scripture is replete with illustrations of how God used committed men and women to represent Him in the political arena. One such example is Joseph. He was taken as a captive and servant into the house of Potiphar, an Egyptian who was one of Pharaoh's officials. It was not Joseph's plan to become a leader in this pagan government. Rather, the sovereign plan of God took him into Egypt. Genesis 39 tells that the Lord was with Joseph and gave him success in everything he did. God also gave him favor in

Potiphar's eyes. Potiphar placed Joseph in charge of his household, and he entrusted to his care everything he owned. Because Joseph lived a righteous life in his master's home, the Lord blessed Potiphar's entire household.

Through a remarkable series of events, God placed Joseph in the position of influencing Pharaoh, the highest official in all Egypt. Even when God's message was not a pleasant one (seven years of famine were coming), Joseph spoke out courageously to the ruler of the land. When Pharaoh discovered that Joseph was the only one who had a plan to prepare Egypt for the great famine, Joseph was put in charge of the palace and assigned to administrate and carry out the entire plan. Joseph's willingness to be used of God in the king's palace resulted in the salvation of thousands of lives, and eventually, in a blessing for all of his own people.

Throughout the monarchial period of Judah's history, God raised up men to provide spiritual and moral guidance for the kings. During a dark period of time, during which the laws of the land had been enacted without regard for God's law, Hilkiah the priest discovered the neglected Book of the Law in the temple. He took it to Shaphan, one of King Josiah's aides, who took it directly to the king. When Josiah heard the words of the Book of the Law, he immediately called together all the people of Judah. He led them in renewing their covenant to follow the Lord and keep His commands.

As the New Testament period opens, we see John the Baptist boldly proclaiming the Kingdom of God as a contrast to the corruption of the political and ecclesiastical structures of his day. He went so far as to rebuke King Herod for living with Herodias, the wife of Herod's brother Philip. Herodias was offended and convicted by John's stand against her immorality. So she prevailed upon the king to behead the prophet. Involvement for God in the political arena was costly for John the Baptist. But it was worthwhile because the standard of God's righteousness was upheld.

Hebrews 11 pays tribute to many men of faith who subdued kingdoms and wrought righteousness, regardless of the personal cost.

In stark contrast to these men of righteousness and faith stands a man who refused to take a stand for God and pay the price of personal involvement. You remember that Abraham's nephew, Lot, chose to move his family into the wicked city of Sodom, a city that glorified every manner of moral perversion. Genesis 19 indicates that Lot achieved some measure of prominence among his fellow citizens in the depraved city. Yet, rather than salting the city with a godly influence, Lot became weak, worldly, and selfish. He never influenced his friends toward righteousness; he failed to exert moral leadership in the hour of crisis. And so, God was forced to utterly destroy the entire city in order that His righteousness and justice might be upheld.

Contemporary Examples of Political Involvement.

Christian political involvement is not limited to biblical days. Most of the great spiritual awakenings in history have influenced Christians to take more seriously their responsibility to shape the moral and social structures of their nation.

A leading denominational journal referred to the 1905 American Awakening as a "Revival of Civic Righteousness." Editorials in other journals spoke of the results of this revival in addressing the moral sins of the day: "So completely have the principles of righteousness permeated the common thought and feeling that even the long tolerated forms of stock gambling and swindling rate-methods have come in for exposure and sharp censure...Preachers are more courageous in their utterances...Men are coming to see that the safety of society and the stability of our free institutions depend upon civic righteousness..."

"Throughout the Republic, there are signs of the revival of the public conscience which, in many states and cities, has broken party lines, rejected machine-made candidates and elected Governors, Senators, Assemblymen, Mayors and County Attorneys of recognized honesty and independence...first fruits of a new zeal for the living Christ as the Lord of all human activity... social, industrial, commercial, and political."

The Dual Citizenship of God's People.

And so, throughout history, God's people have been used as salt to influence government and society to adopt God's moral laws.

We must recognize that Christians have a dual citizenship. First and foremost, we are citizens of God's Kingdom, accountable to all His laws and partakers in all the privileges of His

> # Christian Political Involvement Is Not Limited to Biblical Days.

Kingdom. This is a permanent citizenship. But we also have a temporary citizenship in this earthly nation. God has ordained over the kingdom of earth civil governments, whose responsibility it is to serve Him and to protect the righteous. It is the privilege and responsibility of all Christian Americans to use their influence, whether great or small, to ensure that in all our laws and practices He will have the pre-eminence.

History demonstrates that "when the righteous are in authority, the people rejoice: but when the wicked beareth rule, the people mourn." Turmoil and mourning will always result from choosing wicked men to rule. However, when we choose righteous men who recognize God's sovereignty and are accountable to Him, they will be submissive to and dependent on God, and His righteousness will be exalted in the land and the people will rejoice! But who is going to place the righteous in authority? Will the godless? Will the humanists? No! God-fearing men and women must exercise their privileges and responsibilities as citizens of this nation in order to choose godly representatives and leaders. God's people can make the difference in this nation if they are willing to pay the price of personal involvement, if they are willing to risk anything to raise high in this land the flag of right living. Prayer is part of the price. Respect and obedience are part of the price. And then, as the prophets of old confronted the kings with God's standards, so today, we must take a stand for God. In this great republic we can freely make our voices heard, through writing letters, voting, and informing others when the government makes decisions on moral issues.

Are you willing to be used of God to turn this great nation back to His way? Are you willing to take the responsibility of standing in the gap by involving yourself in the decision making processes of our country? If so, make a commitment to God right now. If you do not know how to get involved, promise Him that you will find out how. If you are fearful of what the cost may be in terms of finances, time or the opinions of others, ask Him for courage. May God bless you as you commit your life to be salt in this rapidly disintegrating nation. And may God bless America and lift high His name in our land, as millions of Christians join together to build up the hedge and stand in the gap.

Republican institutions in the hands of a virtuous and God-fearing nation are the very best in the world, but in the hands of a corrupt and irreligious people they are the very worst and the most effective weapons of destruction....

PHILIP SCHAFF,
CHURCH AND STATE IN THE
UNITED STATES, 1888.

WHY CHRISTIANS SHOULD GET INVOLVED: ANSWERS TO OBJECTIONS

When Christians cease to influence the order of society, that society is left to flounder unprotected amidst the philosophy of the world.

Any man or woman who is willing to stand up and be counted for God is certain to face opposition from many sources. Following are some of the arguments to be faced and God's answer from the Bible.

1. " 'Separation of church and state' prohibits my involvement as a Christian trying to influence public policy."

There is ample historical evidence to prove that the original intent of our founding fathers is exactly what they wrote in the First Amendment to the Constitution and not what our courts and legislators have interpreted it to mean in recent years. Our forefathers were adamant that government (the "state") not be permitted to: (1) establish a federal, "state" religion, or (2) prohibit the free exercise of religion (according to the dictates of the individual conscience).

Today, the secular humanists with their liberal idealogy have been successful in twisting the concept of the separation of church and state to mean separation of God from government. They have convinced us that the church should not expose corruption and immoral legislation, and that Christians should not be active in "politics." They insist that the moral standards of God's law have no bearing on the laws of our land. Yet the government has asserted its control over the churches!

Actually, the Supreme Court and our Congress have violated the guarantees of the First Amendment! Though forbidden from establishing a "state" religion, the federal government is subsidizing the public schools of our nation with millions of tax dollars to teach "humanism," which is defined as a religion in a 1961 Supreme Court ruling! Also, though forbidden to prohibit the free exercise of religion, our Supreme Court and Congress have outlawed prayer and Bible reading from our schools, which used the Bible as the primary textbook from their inception.

The First Amendment was required by the states in order to limit the power of the federal government, and to prevent it from establishing a national denominational church, such as existed in England.

It was designed to protect state-established churches or state-preferred Christian denominations, since at the time of the First Amendment in 1791 over one-third of the thirteen colonies had established churches.

The phrase "wall of separation" is not found in the Constitution, nor is the term "church and state." Thomas Jefferson used the phrase "wall of separation between church and state" in a letter written in 1802.

In his 1805 inaugural address, Jefferson clarified that this statement referred to the separation between the church and the Federal government.

Thomas Jefferson's "wall of separation" phrase has not only been grossly misinterpreted in its original context, but it has now been tragically misapplied to mean separation of God from government.

2. "...Politics are dirty; therefore Christians should not be involved in politics."

In itself, the political process is not "dirty." It has been corrupted by wicked, sinful men and by the neglect of God's people to be the moral conscience of our leaders. Your active participation in the process is not an option, but rather a mandate as a citizen and as a Christian. If this government of the people, by the people, for the people, is to function properly, every citizen has a responsibility to register, vote, be informed, and actively influence others. Jesus commanded His followers to render to Caesar that which was Caesar's. That includes paying our taxes, praying for those in authority over us, and actively speaking out and standing for God and His laws in government.

This is not a matter of "going into politics," but rather fighting the spiritual war where Satan is active—in the political arena. "...We wrestle not against flesh and blood, but against principalities,

against powers ...against spiritual wickedness in high places." Satan would like to use human government to stamp out the testimony and Gospel of Jesus Christ around the world. It is our responsibility to "occupy until Jesus comes."

All of our laws, until recently, were based on biblical law. Today, our legislators are legislating immorality, and we as Christians are endorsing them with our silence. It is time for us to go into the valley (political arena) in the name of Jehovah (whose name is blasphemed and whose laws are scorned) and slay Goliath (humanistic liberalism in our government).

Abraham Lincoln said, "He who affects public sentiment does a far greater service to society than he who enacts statutes." May God help us affect public sentiment to honor God and once again follow His commandments while we still have the freedom to do so.

3. "...The Old Testament promises, which refer to Israel, cannot be applied to America."

America is not the "new Israel" and thereby the recipient of all of God's promises to the nation of Israel. However, the underlying principles of God's dealings with Israel are applicable to America because His ways are based on His unchanging character and attributes. He is the same yesterday, today, and forever.

God's Word declares that the rain falls on the unjust as well as the just. His universal principles apply to all men and nations regardless of their form of government, whether a theocracy, democracy, totalitarian state, dictatorship or a republic. Though God does have a special plan for Israel, His principles will work for any nation or people. Even as a lost man's business is blessed when he honors God with the first fruits of his labor, so also a nation is blessed as she acknowledges her dependence upon God and obeys His commands. Obedience brings blessing; disobedience brings conflict. Though many of our founding fathers did not have a personal relationship with Jesus Christ, they nonetheless honored God, acknowledged His existence and authority and built our early documents and laws on the principles of Scripture. As a result, God blessed America and elevated her in 200 short years from infancy to world leadership.

"Righteousness exalteth a nation..."

In the last 20 years, America has forgotten God, forsaken His commandments and followed the gods of money sex, and humanism. As a result, America is facing the judgment of God militarily, economically, and morally. Jeremiah 18:7-10 says, "At what instant I shall speak concerning a nation, and concerning a kingdom, to pluck up, and to pull down, and to destroy it; If that nation, against whom I have pronounced, turn from their evil, I will repent of the evil that I thought to do unto them. And at what instant I shall speak concerning a nation, and concerning a kingdom, to build and to plant it; If it do evil in my sight, that it obey not my voice, then I will repent of the good, wherewith I said I would benefit them."

4. "...Jesus and the apostles never tried to change the Roman government."

We are not trying to change the American government. But we are responsible as citizens to be active in the process that gives us a voice. Legislation is increasingly affecting every aspect of society. As Christians, we must be active in the political process if God's moral standards are to be reflected in our society.

Jesus and Paul lived under the totalitarian Roman government. For them to have attempted to change their government politically would have been treason. Peter cried, "We ought to obey God rather than men." Jesus' followers never compromised their message, or backed down in their stand for God's truth, even though it eventually cost them their lives at the hand of the Roman government. On the other hand, as Americans, we live in a democratic republic—a government of the people, by the people, for the people. The decisions of our officials are to be a reflection of the convictions of the people. For us not be actively involved and vocally heard is treason against God and His Word.

God intended for Christians to be the "salt of the world," to have a preserving influence on our nation, holding it back from moral spoilage and decay. Throughout history, God has raised up individuals to represent Him in the political arena. Today, we must stand up for God in our democratic republic, using the voice He has granted us. The ungodly cannot be expected to elect righteous officials and to enact legislation based on God's laws. But God's people can make the difference in this nation if they are willing to pay the price of personal involvement.

"The only thing necessary for the triumph of evil is for good men to do nothing."

Edmund Burke

CHARTING A NEW COURSE

The way of action for the involved Christian is marked brightly on the road ahead.

God's people can make the difference in this nation if they are willing to pay the price of personal involvement and if they are willing to risk anything to raise high in this land the flag of right living.

Our freedom to serve God and to promote the gospel in America and around the world is in jeopardy. We must take seriously our responsibility to put God first, not only in our homes and churches, but in our national affairs as well.

How faithfully are you fulfilling these basic duties of every Christian citizen?

1. Pray.

Pray that God will provide for the rule of the godly. Pray that He will change or remove godless and carnal men from positions of leadership. Pray that He will provide for the healing of our land. Pray that He will bring this nation back to the moral principles upon which it was founded. Most importantly, pray that you will do your part and that you will not be discouraged, but that you will continue in the battle. Ask God to make your life an example of obedience to His Word.

Constantly keep your mind on the goal: an America that reflects God's principles in her homes, in her schools, in her communities, in her foreign policy, in all that she does.

2. Register.

In order to serve God as a citizen, you must become a regularly participating voter. But you cannot vote until you have registered your name, address, and other important information with the proper authorities.

Many millions of God's people throughout America are not even registered to vote. How can we as Christian citizens expect God to restore righteous leadership through us, unless we are willing to take a few minutes to register? Only when you have registered to vote will you be in a position to help assure the election of godly officials.

Registering to vote is a simple process. Contact your county or city election office, political party headquarters, or even your local library. They can give you information on where and how to register.

3. Become Informed.

Once you have registered, you assume a responsibility to use your vote wisely. Just as the untrained soldier is at the mercy of his enemy, the uninformed Christian is incapable of prevailing against the forces of evil in the world of politics. In order to serve God effectively as a citizen of our country, you must know how to utilize the existing political processes for His glory.

Do not be overwhelmed! The range of issues and concerns is so broad that you cannot effectively know them all. Pick one issue cluster, and make it "your" issue area. Say it is education reform, or pornography, or a godly national defense. Arrange with your friends that they will pick other issues as theirs, so that you can be sure of knowing when your action can help other issues as well.

Read articles on your subject in the newspapers, in Christian magazines, and in secular magazines. Go to the public library and read what liberal magazines say about your issue. Watch the political discussion shows on T.V. To be truly informed you must know what those who think differently say about your issue— only then can you effectively defend your cause.

Find out who are the elected officials who are in a position to influence your issue. If your issue is pornography, and your goal is a city ordinance restricting pornography, you must learn about and meet your city council members. You would want to learn about, and meet, your local U.S. attorney—you will perhaps want to encourage him to initiate a prosecution of pornography. If your concern is education, you must learn about the members of your local school board, and the State Board of Education, and the Education Committees in your State Legislature. If your concern is national defense, you have "only" the

Federal level to worry about: the Armed Services committees in the House and Senate, the policies of the Defense Department, and—especially important— the dispositions of the members of Congress from your district and other districts in the state.

You must follow the process of legislation you are concerned with; communicate with other like-minded people about your issue of concern; communicate with your elected representatives, local, state, or federal, as appropriate, to express your concerns and ask their vote; encourage other like-minded persons to communicate with their elected representatives.

If you are not able to head up an "issues cluster group," then let those who are heading up such groups know that you are willing to help them. Tell them to ask for your help when it is needed. Perhaps a Civic Affairs Committee of your church should give regular reports to the entire church.

Contact your local library, party headquarters, and pro-life and pro-family groups to learn the following basic information:

Candidates for federal, state, and local elections. Explanation of American party system and election process. Update on laws being enacted by legislative bodies.

The resource list at the end of this book contains much valuable information about how to be better informed on the various issues confronting our nation today.

4. Contact Your Elected Officials.

Write or call your elected officials when an issue requires to express your opinions and concerns on moral issues and legislation. Various publications (see resource list) will keep you informed of major national legislation that you should support or oppose. Even a simple postcard to the appropriate official can be effective. Phone calls to the local office of a congressman or Senator are particularly effective. It will let him know that the godly people in his district do care and are aware of his activities.

5. Seek Out and Support Good Candidates.

The men and women who run for office and support moral issues need your help. There are any number of things you can do to help them. You can hold a coffee for them and invite the members of your church to attend. You can write a letter on their behalf to your congregation. You can help on a phone bank for them, and you can contribute money to their campaign. You cannot do everything—but you can do something!

6. Attend Your Political Party's Precinct and Committee Meetings.

Bring like-minded, God-fearing people with you and do not be afraid to speak out.

At these meetings, people are selected as delegates for county and state meetings. In most states, the county and state meetings will adopt a platform. In some states, they will elect delegates to the national conventions, which will select the party candidates for President, and in others they will select the candidates who run for state-wide office. In the latter states, it is even more important that you attend the meetings.

7. Vote.

Just one vote? With millions of voters voting, how can just one vote be important? Well, every year in this nation hundreds of elections are won or lost by just one vote per precinct! In fact, some have been lost—or won—by less than one vote per precinct!

In 1948, Lyndon B. Johnson was elected to the U.S. Senate by 87 votes out of 988,295 votes cast in 6,000 precincts. That figures out to 1/69th of a vote per precinct!

In 1974, James Rhodes of Ohio defeated incumbent John Gilligan and was elected Governor by a margin of about 10,000 votes; less than one vote in each of Ohio's 12,800 precincts.

In 1960, John F. Kennedy defeated Richard M. Nixon by 113,000 votes. That was about one half vote per precinct!

You must vote in all the elections—primary, general, and special elections. Mark on your calendar the election days so you can be sure to vote. If you are going to be out of town, then be sure to vote by absentee ballot. For absentee ballots, contact your county or city election office.

On election day, you can also help godly candidates by working with their

> ### Vote Your Christian Convictions in Preference to Your Party.

campaign to ensure that their voters go to the polls.

Make a sincere effort to obtain reliable information about all issues and candidates before casting your vote. In making your decision, let the Word of God be your guide. If there is not a qualified candidate who is spiritually mature, vote for one whose personal principles and platform most nearly agree with your own Christian position, based on the Bible. Remember that a candidate's principles are far more important than his party. Vote your Christian convictions in preference to your party.

More than half of the people of the United States profess faith in Jesus Christ. Even a small percentage who will take seriously their responsibility as Christian citizens, can be used of God to set this nation on a new course of righteousness for His glory.

8. Help Your Pastor to Inform Church Members.

Collecting important dates for voter registration, elections, political meetings, dates of major public hearings, etc., are all vitally important for Christian citizens. One of your major contributions can be keeping your pastor and church members informed of these days and dates.

9. Financial Involvement.

Political campaigns and the successful victories on issues require strong financing. What is the money used for? Advertisements are necessary for media use, printing, office facilities, postage, telephones, meeting halls, and room rentals. In addition, there are many organizations that require financial contributions to promote biblical morality

in this country. We must be willing to make financial contributions and encourage our friends and neighbors to do the same.

10. Be willing to Sacrifice Yourself.

When secular politicians count Christian votes, that's fine. But the way to really turn the country around is to elect people who are believers first—before they become politicians. There's a congressman from New Jersey who was a grassroots right-to-life activist long before he thought about running for Congress. He's a real leader in Congress now. The country needs more godly, upright men and women willing to sacrifice themselves to run for and hold public office. Encourage your fellow Christians to make this sacrifice. And if you are asked—don't bury your talent for service through public office. Local offices are easy to win and hold, and they're the first step on the ladder.

Making Your Influence Felt.

In order to make your influence felt, you must know who your leaders are and how to contact them. Officials depend on the vote of the people and they listen to those groups that speak out on the issues. It is important for you to obtain the names, addresses, and telephone numbers of the following elected officials. All this information should be available at your local library, newspaper, or at the county clerk's office.

National Offices
—President of the United States
—U.S. Senators (each state has two)
—U.S. Congressman (from your district)

State Offices

The number of elected state officers and legislators will vary from state to state. In all states, except Nebraska, there is both an upper house and a lower house in the state legislature. At a minimum, you should have the names of the following individuals.

—Governor
—Attorney
—State Senator
—State Representative (Assembly man, or Delegate)

County Officials

(The number and name of elected county officials will vary. The most important ones are those who make policy. This body is usually called the Board of Supervisors.)

—Chairman of the Board
—Supervisor (elected in your district)

City/Town Officials

(Some people do not live in cities or towns and will not have these officials.)

—Mayor
—City/Town Councilman (from your district)

School Boards

(If your school board members are elected, you should give particular attention to these office holders. This is important because of the influence they hold over what is taught to our children.)

—School Board Chairman
—School Board Members

Political Party Officers

(The influence of party officials varies from state to state. Their influence can be most important in states which nominate candidates for offices through conventions or caucuses.)

—County Chairman (of your party)
—Precinct Chairman (of your party)

How to Write Effectively to Your Leaders.

1. Identify Yourself.

Increase you effectiveness by describing yourself as:

a) A constituent or correspondent writing to other congressmen.

b) When writing to other congressmen than your own, be sure and mention the connections that you have (family, friends, or business interests) in the state or district served by them.

c) A voter (also: campaign contributor, precinct worker of either party, etc.)

d) An active citizen (member of civic group, service organization, veterans, or religious organization, etc.)

e) A taxpayer (farmer, union machinist, housewife, businessman, stockholder, homeowner, etc.)

2. Be Friendly.

Letters from thoughtful friends or undecided voters have more influence than letters from implacable enemies. Leave name-calling and threats to the other side. Remember, you represent the Lord in your words and attitudes.

3. Give Praise.

When your man votes "right," give him a "thanks" and a "keep up the good

> **Remember, You Represent The Lord In Your Words And Attitudes.**

work" even if he usually votes wrong. It is important, because the other side will be heaping abuse on him through the press and their letters at the same time.

4. One Subject Per Letter.

Do not indulge in long letters with many subjects. Write often on separate issues. You will save time, write a more readable letter and multiply your effectiveness this way.

5. Be Neat and Brief.

If possible, type your letter. Otherwise, write or print neatly, to make it easy to read. Your return address must be complete and legible on the letter as well as on the envelope. Write a short opening, two or three paragraphs on the subject and a short closing.

6. Address Properly.

The honorable (full name of senator or representative)
(State) Senate or (State) House of
    Representatives
P.O. Box (Number)
(City), (State) (Zip)
Dear Mr. or Dear Governor (Last name)
Re: Bill No.

7. Know Your Subject.

Know how a piece of legislation violates the principles of God's Word. Identify the legislation by a bill number, unless it has been widely publicized by a particular name. If a particular correction would make the bill more acceptable, describe the change you would like to see adopted and why.

8. Be Specific.

Mention specific arguments, rather than generalities such as "this bill is pure Communism," etc. Being specific

puts pressure on the congressman to be specific in his own reply. Ask the question: "Will you oppose such-and-such an amendment? If not, will you please explain why you will not?" This will sometimes cause the congressman to seriously consider an issue for the first time.

9. Add Weight.

If you are making a report to your church or civic organization on the subject of your letter, say so. You can enclose a clipping from the local newspaper to support the point you make. Be sure to name the paper and the date. Another good way to add weight to your letter is to write a "Letter to the Editor" of the local paper, then enclose a carbon copy together with your letter to the congressman thus letting him know that you are influencing other voters, also.

10. No "Form" Letters.

"Form" letters, or letters copied for "sample" letters show that you are not interested enough to take the time to learn about the issue and write your own feelings on it.

Never mention another person or group (such as your church) as the source of your ideas. This offers the congressman a chance to avoid the issue by attacking the source. Avoid group letters and petitions. Never send a carbon copy alone, but always "cover" it with an original note or letter referring to the carbon copy enclosed.

11. Ask for a Reply.

If no reply is necessary, say so. If you want a reply to a specific question, ask for it. It never hurts to try to get a commitment from your congressman, but

don't be surprised if he avoids committing himself in advance of a vote. He may be honestly undecided and needs more time to consider it. You can take advantage of his indecision as an opportunity to write a second letter on the same subject bringing up new points.

12. Write Often.

Two or three letters per month are not too many. You can cover more subjects that way, and if you keep it brief, each letter will take only a few minutes of your time. Urge others to write.

13. Pray First.

Pray for the one to whom you are writing. Ask God to bind and rebuke Satan for any deception which would cause a rejection of God's principles. Fervent prayer avails much.

THE ELECTION SYSTEM.

How the People in Authority Are Selected.

The election system in most states consists of two levels. The primary election is where the nominees of the parties are selected for the general election. In some states the party nominees are selected through caucuses. However, most states do have primary elections. In these elections the participants are often limited to voters registered in that party. The turnout is usually not as great as in the general election and so the influence of each voter is greater.

The general election is the final contest between the winners of the party primary elections. In these elections, all registered voters may participate and vote for any candidate, regardless of party affiliation. While these elections are important, the voter usually has only two choices. Therefore, it is important to exert your influence long before the general election.

The chart below illustrates the election process.

Primary Election (Round 1)	General Election Winner
Party A	
Joe (5,500)	
Bill (26,000)	
Amy (9,000)	
Bob (27,300)	Bob (85,000)
Party B	
Dave (3,000)	
Max (22,000)	Max (81,000)
Nancy (21,000)	
Party C	
Pete (2,500)	Pete (2,000)

(If you do not participate in the primary election, you have defaulted half the battle!)

Which of These Important Commitments Have You Made?

1. I pray daily for my elected officials, for a spiritual awakening in our nation, and for God's will in critical issues facing this country.

2. I am registered to vote.

3. I know who my elected officials are and I keep informed on key issues and legislation.

4. I regularly write or call my elected officials to express my opinion on moral issues and legislation.

5. I seek out and support good candidates for federal, state, and local office.

6. I attend my political party's precinct and committee meetings.

7. I have joined with other concerned

citizens in my area who are promoting godly morality.

8. I regularly vote in federal, state, and local elections.

9. I help keep my pastor informed on key moral issues and legislation.

10. I contribute financially to candidates and organizations that are promoting biblical morality.

Examine the commitments you have not yet made. Ask God to help you assign them their proper priority. Immediately determine when and how you will fulfill your responsibility in these areas. Then communicate these important steps to others.

❧

I am only one, but I am one. I cannot do everything, but I can do something. What I can do, I should do and, with the help of God, I will do!

EVERETT HALE

SEVEN PRINCIPLES THAT MADE AMERICA GREAT

BY JERRY FALWELL

*The biblical standards of a grand new nation
are desperately needed today.*

In 1789, the first President of these United States, George Washington, spoke with prudence when he said in his first inaugural address, "The propitious smiles of heaven can never be expected on a nation that disregards the eternal rules of order and right which heaven itself has ordained."

In 1796, in leaving what was then, and indeed will be for all time, the highest office in our land, George Washington spoke urgent words of farewell: "Of all the dispositions and habits which lead to political prosperity, religion and morality are indispensable support. In vain would that man claim the tribute of patriotism who should labor to subvert these great pillars."

America has not been, nor ever will be, a great nation because she harbors a wealth of natural resources, or a strategic position among the lands of this earth, or a populace of intellectual elitists. America's greatness will forever expressly parallel her adherence to certain basic principles that were paramount in her inception and that will always continue to be absolutely necessary to her continued existence. God

elevated America to greatness because she adhered to these principles.

America is a nation under God, built upon seven principles of the Judeo-Christian ethic. It is these seven principles that guided the thinking of our founding fathers as they penned the Declaration of Independence and the Constitution. All the compacts, agreements, and statutes on which our federal government and all 50 state governments are predicated are based on these principles.

Enumerated, these Old and New Testament biblical principles include:

1. *The principle of the dignity of human life* (Exodus 20:13; Matthew 5:21,22).

The Bible clearly points out, "Thou shalt not kill (commit murder)." In a land that has led the world in its position regarding the dignity and value of human life, we are today allowing the murder of millions of innocent babies. Our Supreme Court has ruled that innocent and defenseless unborn babies have no right to live. We are blatantly and shamelessly violating a moral principle upon which this nation was built, and we are suffering the consequences of this violation.

2. *The principle of the traditional monogamous family (Genesis 2:21-24; Ephesians 5:22-33).*

A family begins when a man legally marries a woman. Diverse family forms such as common law marriage or homosexual marriage are not acceptable. They are an abomination to God who divinely ordained order in the family relationship.

3. *The principle of common decency (Genesis 3:7,21; Matthew 5:27,28; Ephesians 5:3-5).*

Common decency in a race that is fallen because of sin begins with the covering of the human body. Today pornography is a four-billion-dollar business in our country. Lewd magazines portraying filthy acts are sold on newsstands at the eye level of a five-year-old child. Television programs and movies are filled with vulgarity, profanity, and obscenity.

4. *The principle of the work ethic (Genesis 3:19; Exodus 20:9,10; II Thessalonians 3:10).*

The Bible makes it clear that a man is to live by working with his hands. The result of the curse of sin upon man was that by the sweat of his brow he would earn his bread. There is a dignity in hard work, a dignity the welfare system has stripped from millions of Americans. The free enterprise system encourages ambition, incentive, competition, and hard work.

5. *The principle of the Abrahamic covenant (Genesis 12:1-3; Romans 11:1,2).*

Several thousand years ago God told Abraham that out of his seed would come a great nation, more numerous than the stars in the heaven and the sands of the seashore. God promised Abraham that through his seed all the families of the earth would be blessed. This is the Messianic Promise. Jesus Christ provided the fulfillment for that blessing. Although all people are equally loved by God, Jews, are God's chosen people. Palestine belongs to Israel. God deals with nations in relation to how those nations deal with Israel.

6. *The principle of God-centered education (Deuteronomy 6:4-9; Ephesians 6:4).*

In recent years, the name of Almighty God has literally been removed from our public schools. Voluntary prayer has been banned. Creationism is no longer taught as a viable alternative to evolution which is now taught as a fact. As God was taken out of our schools, we saw moral permissiveness, academic deterioration, and the drug epidemic creep in.

In many cases, sex education classes in the public school are nothing more than academic pornography. Secular humanism, rather than God-centered education, has resulted in decadence and deterioration.

7. *The principle of divinely ordained establishments.*

A. The home (Genesis 2:21-24; Ephesians 5:22-23). B. State or civil government (Genesis 10:32; Romans 13:1-7). C. Religious institution (Exodus 25:8,9-tabernacle/temple Matthew 16:17-19).

God divinely ordained the institutions of the home, the state (civil government), and the church.

The home is the basic unit of a civilized society. A society is only as strong as the homes within that society.

Since God established human, civil government, to rebel against government, except when government rebels against God, is to rebel against God Himself. We are to respect authority and pray for our leaders.

God established the church, and though it has always been under direct attack by Satan, it will always remain strong and triumphant. It must always sound forth the clear Gospel message: Jesus Christ was crucified, He was buried, He rose from the dead three days later, triumphant over death, hell, and the grave. He is seated at the right hand of God and will redeem all who come to Him in simple, childlike faith.

We need a return to God and to the Bible as never before in the history of America. Undoubtedly we are at the edge of eternity. Some are already referring to us as "post-Christian America." We have stretched the rubber band of morality too far already. A few more stretches and it will undoubtedly snap forever. When that happens we will become like all the other nations preceding us who've fallen under the judgment of God.

It is time to call America back to her moral roots. It is time to call America back to God. We need a revival of righteous living based on a proper confession of sin and repentance of heart if we are to remain the land of the free and the home of the brave!

I am convinced that God is calling millions of Americans in the so-often silent majority to join in the crusade to turn America around in our lifetime. Let us unite our hearts and lives together for the cause of a new America... a moral America in which righteousness will exalt this nation. Only as we do this can we exempt ourselves from one day having to look our children in the eyes and answer this searching question: "Mom and Dad, where were you the day freedom died in America?"

WHICH WAY,

"One nation...under God!"

What does this mean?

It means that we have this land, this flag,
    this government as a gift from the Great God
    Almighty.

It means that this did not become
    "the land of the free and the home of the brave"
    by blind fate or a happy set of coincidences,
    but that a wise and benevolent God was hovering
    over us from the very hour of conception...
    and long before.

When Columbus discovered this Land,
    he took a cross in his own hands,
    and planted it upon the new soil,
    fell upon his knees, and kissing the earth,
    took possession of this continent for God.

Faith in God hung the lanterns on the prow of the
    "Mayflower" as it charted the treacherous Atlantic.

That frail vessel was laden with deathless destiny:
    The pioneers of a powerful nation...
    the heralds of new freedoms...
    the trailblazers of a new epoch in human history.

Later, during those difficult but decisive days of
    the Revolution when a handful of common people
    won their freedom from a mighty world empire,
    through the crucible of a Civil War, through
    two World Wars and a number of smaller wars,
    through a great panic and a ravaging depression,
    none but the fool could fail to see the hand of
    a sovereign God upon this golden land of the free.

But today America faces a danger point.

We must confess with troubled heart that America
    has forgotten God.

She is rolling in luxuries, reveling in excesses,
    rollicking in pleasure, revolting in morals,
    and rotting in sin.

What can we expect of a society in which passions
    are riderless horses:

AMERICA?

in which there is a desolation of decency;
in which love has become a jungle emotion,
lust is exalted to lordship,
sin elevated to sovereignty,
Satan worshipped as a saint,
and man magnified above his Maker?

Today, the bleak winds of destiny are howling in
protest to the way we are living.

It is sheer folly to suppose that the strength and
security of America
lies in its vast economic resources...
industrial prowess...
scientific ingenuity...
diplomatic skill or military might.

Our real defense as a nation rests in the spiritual
convictions,
character and commitment
of our citizenry.

Our forefathers founded this nation upon the
Christian faith and it will live so long as the Lord
is our God.

The Pilgrim Fathers left a land where they were
persecuted to find a land wherein every man,
through countless ages, would have the right to
worship God in his own way.

When these strong and stalwart champions of a new
order landed at Plymouth Rock, they knelt upon
the shore and dedicated this country to God.

When the Constitutional Convention met at
Philadelphia to organize the nation and write a
constitution, venerable old Benjamin Franklin
called on the members of the Convention to fall
upon their knees and pray for divine wisdom.

Today, as of old, each of the coins of our pockets
bears the inscription,
"In God we trust."

This same principle of dependence upon God is
embodied in our National Anthem:

"Blest with victory and peace,
May the heaven-rescued land,
Praise the Power that hath made
And preserved us a nation!

Sin separates a nation from God!

Sin separates this nation from God!

But we are not without hope.

I agree that the picture has a dark background but I
would like to place a crimson cross and bursting
tomb and a glowing sky in the foreground.

From the very throne of God there comes this
message to us:
"Come now, and let us reason together,
saith the Lord: though your sins be as scarlet,
they shall be as white as snow:
though they be red like crimson,
they shall be as wool."

We must return to the Faith of our Fathers.

We must go to our knees in humility and prayer,
in contrition and confession,
in repentance and the forsaking of sin.

We must go back to the cross,
where the incarnate Son of God was cursed,
condemned, crucified for man—the creature's sin.

The crisis is acute.

The danger is imminent.

Time is running out.

Something miraculous must happen in the heart
and soul of America...
now, before it is too late.

The choice is clear.

It is repent or perish,
revival or ruin,
Christ or chaos.
The question of the hour is: Which Way, America?

A NATION REBORN:
A Conclusion.

"Born again" has become a catch phrase of our generation. It is applied to an incredible array of things and endeavors. One newscast refers to a resurging sports team as being "born again." A do-it-yourself magazine tells how to have a "born again" attic! The once-cursed Chrysler Corporation is dubbed a "born again" industrial giant. So the list goes on, and how unfortunate, for this beautiful term has been taken out of context, maligned and misused.

Who coined this phrase, anyway? And what did he mean by it? The originator, of course, was Jesus. He utilized this expression one evening when he was approached by a prominent man named Nicodemus. An esteemed Jewish lawyer, Nicodemus came to Jesus seeking spiritual counsel. Jesus' seemingly nonsensical response was, "Except a man be born again, he cannot see the kingdom of God."

Be born again? "How is this possible?" Nicodemus asked. Jesus replied that just as one is born physically, he must be born spiritually. And he added for emphasis, "Marvel not...ye must be born again."

The only true rebirth is spiritual in nature. It is experienced when one turns in genuine faith and repentance to Jesus Christ and receives His free gift of salvation.

How then can a nation be reborn? Clearly it is not possible nor plausible that everyone in this or any other country would voice a collective prayer of faith and repentance. But national rebirth can occur when a great number of individuals turn to God. Such has been the case in the noted spiritual awakenings of past generations.

The answer to life's deepest needs is not to be found in better education, good government, profitable commerce, or any other dimension of this world. Only in Christ is there hope, for any person and any nation.

The Rebirth of America is not a noble aspiration. It is a desperate need and, by God's grace, may become a glorious reality, at this crucial hour.

The next few pages may be the most important pages of this entire book.

It is easy to look at our nation's rich Christian heritage and the extent of our spiritual and moral decline, and to feel overwhelmed by the massive rebuilding effort that will be required to restore America's foundations. The temptation is to surrender to the seeming hopelessness of the task and to sit back and do nothing. And that is exactly what we must *not* do.

The need is for each of us to do *something*. As you have read this book, chances are that you have been particularly challenged by one or two topics. The Resource List that follows will give you a place to start in dealing with your special concerns.

Under each category are listed selected books, newsletters, and organizations that address that specific concern. This resource list is by no means exhaustive. There are many other helpful re-sources available that have not been included, due either to space limitations, or because the publishers were not aware of them.

Before putting this book down, why not take time to read the list in the area of your greatest interest. Then determine a few, simple specific steps of action. Select one book that you would like to read. Write or call an organization and ask if they have a chapter in your area. Ask how you can get involved in their efforts. Subscribe to a newsletter or publication in your area of interest.

Begin *now* the process of becoming better informed and involved as a part of the solution.

RESOURCES

ABORTION/HUMAN LIFE

PUBLICATIONS:

Burtchaell, James Tunstead, *Rachel Weeping.* Fairway, KS: Andrews and McMeel, 1986.

This book is a storehouse of invaluable information—biological, medical, ethical, sociological—establishing beyond a doubt that human life begins at conception and documenting the havoc resulting from *Roe vs. Wade.* The book clearly and exhaustively details the parallels between the language, attitudes, and mentality of slavery and the Nazi holocaust, and those of the proabortion forces in America.

Garton, Jean, *Who Broke the Baby?* Minneapolis: Bethany Fellowship, 1979.

A mere glance at photographs of aborted fetuses was enough to convince Dr. Garton's young child that a baby had been "broken." This book explores the horror of abortion in the twentieth century and how it has become a catastrophe ignored.

Koop, C. Everett, M.D., *The Right to Live: The Right to Die.* Wheaton, IL: Tyndale House Publishers, 1976.

The Surgeon General of the United States discusses the social movement that undermines the value of human life and results in abortion, infantacide, and ultimately, euthanasia.

Nathanson, Bernard, M.D., *Aborting America.* Toronto: Life Cycle Books, 1979.

A well-known obstetrician and gynecologist, Dr. Nathanson presided over 60,000 abortions before he came to believe abortion on request is wrong. This book is about the evolution of his beliefs and the effect the repeal of abortion laws had on the United States and on medicine.

Reagan, Ronald, *Abortion and the Conscience of the Nation.* Nashville: Thomas Nelson Publishers, 1984.

President Ronald Reagan has said, "Since 1973, more than 15 million unborn children have had their lives snuffed out by legalized abortions. That is over ten times the number of Americans lost in all our nation's wars." In his book, President Reagan explains the consequences abortion has on the entire moral fabric of society.

Schaeffer, Francis and C. Everett Koop, M.D., *Whatever Happened to the Human Race?* Old Tappan, NJ: Fleming H. Revell, 1979.

Includes definitive statements about abortion, infanticide, euthanasia and what this destruction of human life means to us and to future generations. The final chapter suggests a plan for action.

Willke, John C., M.D., *Handbook on Abortion.* Cincinnati: Hayes Publishing Company, 1971.

Dr. John Willke is a leading authority on abortion and the pro-life movement. This book provides an excellent overview of the situation today.

ORGANIZATIONS:

American Life League
Box 490
Stafford, VA 22554
(703) 659-4171

The primary goals of the American Life League include the passage of the Human Life Amendment to restore the sanctity of life to all human beings, born and preborn; the elimination of value-free "sex instruction" programs in education; and opposition to anti-life organizations, i.e., those which fund "family planning" programs that encourage abortions, sterilizations and the use of abortifacient drugs and/or devices. The monthly news magazine, *A.L.L. About Issues,* covers current legislative and government activities with articles on a wide variety of topics of concern to the pro-life, pro-family movement. A.L.L. has an active presence on Capitol Hill.

Americans United for Life
230 North Michigan Avenue
Suite 915
Chicago, Illinois 60601
(312) 263-5029

Americans United for Life is a national legal and educational pro-life organization. The AUL Legal Defense Fund provides legal information and resources to decision makers, elected officials, and concerned citizens nationwide, and becomes involved in selected cases with implications for the pro-life movement. Publications include *Lex Vitae,* a regular update on legal

happenings in the life issues (free for the first six months), *AUL Newsletter* (free for first six months); and *AUL Studies* ($1.00 per copy).

Christian Action Council
701 West Broad St. #405
Falls Church, VA 22046
(703) 237-2100

The Christian Action Council is a pro-life organization committed to the passage of a Human Life Amendment which will effectively end abortion on demand in America. The CAC is helping local churches to establish Crisis Pregnancy Centers for women with problem pregnancies, offering them real alternatives to abortion. Pamphlets "Abortion on Demand?" and "Abortion: Providing Alternatives" and the *Action Line* newsletter are available free upon request.

The Human Life Foundation
150 East 35th Street
New York, NY 10016

Publishes quarterly the *Human Life Review,* which presents fine articles on abortion, euthanasia, experimentation on living subjects, and many other "life" issues. For a year's subscription, send $15.00 to the Human Life Foundation.

Liberty Godparent Ministry
P.O. Box 27000
Lynchburg, VA 24506
(804) 847-6806
The Liberty Godparent Ministry specializes in providing free room and board, professional counseling services, pregnancy testing and adoption services to women with an unplanned pregnancy. It also provides information on how churches or groups of concerned

individuals can begin such ministries. Write to Executive Director Jim Savley for details.

National Right to Life Committee
419 Seventh Street, NW Suite 402
Washington, DC 20004
(202) 626-8800

The National Right to Life Committee seeks passage of pro-life legislation and has over 2000 local right-to-life groups nationwide. NRLC publishes a biweekly newspaper called *NRL News* (sample copy available upon request). It has an active Capitol Hill presence.

ECONOMICS

PUBLICATIONS:

Burkett, Larry, *Your Finances in Changing Times.* Chicago: Moody Press, 1975.
Deals with present economy, biblical principles, and practical applications.

Davis, John Jefferson, *Your Wealth in God's World.* Phillipsburg, NJ: Presbyterian and Reformed Publishing Company, 1984.
Davis defends the biblical morality of the free-market system vs. a coercive state-led economic system. He shows that economics is a moral issue with obvious religious roots. The book answers the attack of "left-wing" evangelicalism on the free-market system.

Friedman, Milton and Rose Friedman, *Free to Choose.* New York: Harcourt Brace Jovanovich, 1979.

Gilder, George, *Wealth and Poverty.* New York: Basic Books, 1981.

Gilder shows how the essence of capitalism is not greed as many claim but is giving. He makes a case for the moral as well as the practical merits of capitalism.

Griffiths, Brian, *The Creation of Wealth: A Christian's Case for Capitalism.* Downers Grove, IL: Intervarsity Press, 1984.
Brian Griffiths considers the economic, theological, ethical, and ideological dimensions of creating wealth. While he finds that some capitalism is shot through with humanistic values, he believes a capitalism based on biblical principles offers the best hope for using our resources wisely and meeting the needs of the world.

Kirk, Russell, *The Conservative Mind.* Chicago: Regenery, 1953.
A basic history of conservative economic thought which is based on Orthodox Judeo-Christian tradition.

Lindsell, Harold, *Free Enterprise: A Judeo-Christian Defense.* Wheaton, IL: Tyndale House Publishers, 1982.
Develops the biblical concept of private property and shows its applicability for today. Also shows that socialism is contrary to the commandment "Thou shalt not steal."

Rose, Tom, *Economics: The American Economy.* Mercer, PA: American Enterprise Publications, 1985.

Schaeffer, Franky (ed.), *Is Capitalism Christian? Toward a Christian Perspective on Economics.* Westchester, IL: Crossway Books, 1985.
Brings together in one volume the West's leading economic, political, and social writers and clearly shows that

hope for the Third World lies not in socialism or communism but in the freedom and economic opportunity provided by democratic capitalism.

Sproul, R.C. Jr., *Money Matters.* Wheaton, IL: Tyndale House Publishers, 1985.

R.C. Sproul, Jr. offers original insights and clear teaching about inflation, profit, taxation, free enterprise, socialism, and materialism. Furthermore, *Money Matters* explores what the Bible says about economic policy and suggests what you can do about economics at the national level.

EDUCATION

PUBLICATIONS:

Barton, John and John Whitehead, *Schools on Fire.* Wheaton IL: Tyndale House, 1980.

In 1963 the Supreme Court did not outlaw Christianity from the public school classrooms. But if the court ruled against the teaching *of* religion, it just as strongly urged the teaching *about* religion. It warned that an educational system "cleansed" of religious value becomes instead the purveyor of a secular faith. That is exactly what happened.

Hefley, James C., *Textbooks on Trial.* Wheaton, IL: Victor Books, 1976.

An informative report of Mel and Norma Gabler's ongoing battle against humanism in public school.textbooks.

LaHaye, Tim, *The Battle for the Public Schools.* Old Tappan, NJ: Fleming H. Revell, 1982.

An examination of the development and direction of public schools with emphasis on the apparent direction they are leading us as a nation.

Macaulay, Susan Schaeffer, *For the Children's Sake.* Westchester, IL: Crossway Books, 1984.

Every parent and teacher wants to give their children the best education possible. Everyone would like education to be a joyous celebration of life, as well as a solid preparation for living. Sadly, most education today falls far short of this goal. But, as Susan Schaeffer Macaulay shows, it doesn't have to be this way. *For the Children's Sake* is a book about what education can be—for your child, in your home, and in your school.

McGuffey, William H., *The McGuffey Readers.* New York: American Book Company, 1896.

If America's schools were different one hundred years ago, perhaps part of the reason is because the textbooks were different! The *McGuffey Readers* are still valuable today.

Morris, Barbara, *Change Agents in the Schools.* Upland, CA: Barbara Morris Report, 1979.

Presents the goals of secular humanism and the methods being used in the schools to accomplish these goals.

Morris, Henry, *Education for the Real World.* San Diego: Creation Life Publishers, 1977.

Places education in its true biblical perspective, preparing people for fruitful lives in both time and eternity.

ORGANIZATIONS:

Educational Research Analysts
Mel and Norma Gabler
Box 7518
Longview, TX 75607
(214) 753-5993

Since 1961, Mel and Norma Gabler have become well-known conservative critics of the public education system in America. Norma regularly appears before the Texas committee and boards which approve texts. The Gablers have been instrumental in encouraging groups and individuals to work toward keeping humanistic textbooks out of the schools. Information on the Gabler's textbook review library is available upon request. Reviews and other materials are furnished on a contribution basis.

FAMILY

PUBLICATIONS:

Christenson, Larry, *The Christian Family.* Minneapolis: Bethany Fellowship, 1978.

Shows God's order for the family and the family's relationship to Jesus Christ.

Hancock, Maxine, *Love, Honor, and Be Free.* Chicago: Moody Press, 1975.

Handford, Elizabeth Rice, *Me? Obey Him?* Murfreesboro, TN: Sword of the Lord Publishers, 1972.

Deals with an area fraught with opinion and prejudice—a wife's submission to her husband. Should she obey in everything? Mrs. Handford deals with this question and many others with remarkable clarity and scriptural evidence.

Horton, Marilee, *Free to Stay at Home: A Woman's Alternative.* Waco, TX: Word Books, 1982

In her witty and amusing style, Marilee Horton explains the pressures women face to join the work force and find meaning for life outside motherhood and the traditional role.

Jepsen, Dee, *Beyond Equal Rights.* Waco, TX Word Books, 1984.

Dee Jepsen, former Special Assistant to the President for Public Liaison to women's organizations, is concerned about the needs of women in all walks of life. This book explains why women's problems have been only partially solved by legislation and why women have difficulty in discovering their true identity and self-worth.

Kramer, Rita, *In Defense of the Family.* New York: Basic Books, 1983.

Rita Kramer understands the feminist movement and its anti-family propaganda. She sets forth a compelling argument for the pro-family point of view that promotes the idea of women putting their children and home as a "number one priority" ahead of career, money, and superficial prestige.

LaHaye, Tim, *Battle for the Family.* Old Tappan, NJ: Fleming H. Revell Company, 1983.

Identification of 15 major ways in which humanism infiltrates the home and family. Offers suggestions for winning the battle for your family.

MacDonald, Gordon, *Magnificent Marriage.* Wheaton, IL: Tyndale House, 1976.

The author has drawn on his own marriage, his pastoral encounters, and his insight into the Bible to give a down-to-earth view of what marriage is and can be. MacDonald demonstrates that a successful marriage consists of a balance of four essential elements: romance, companionship, service, and sexuality.

Petersen, J. Allen, *The Myth of the Greener Grass.* Wheaton, IL: Tyndale House, 1983.

A family counselor speaks frankly about extramarital affairs and offers both preventive and healing measures.

Ray, Bruce A., *Withhold Not Correction.* Phillipsburg, NJ: Presbyterian and Reformed Publishing, 1978.

How should children be disciplined? Bruce Ray explains the loving and firm method of discipline espoused in the Bible.

Ryrie, Charles and Paul Steele, *Meant to Last.* Wheaton, IL: Victor Books, 1983.

There is hope for the divorce generation. Our hope lies in conforming to God's standards for marriage, divorce, and remarriage. The author examines God's standards as revealed in His Word.

Schaeffer, Edith, *What Is a Family?* Old Tappan, NJ: Fleming H. Revell, 1975.

You'll enjoy this creative woman's insights as she shares the principles behind loving family living.

Schlafly, Phyllis, *The Power of the Positive Woman.* New Rochelle, NY: Arlington House, 1977.

The Positive Woman asserts her right to be a *woman* and her power to nurture life, to build a home, to achieve on womanly terms, to inspire and lead others, and to bring love, beauty, and happiness to herself and those around her. Simply being a unisex "person" is not as liberating as following God's design.

Wheat, Ed, *Love Life for Every Married Couple.* Grand Rapids: Zondervan, 1980.

Dr. Wheat explains how you can fall in love, stay in love, and rekindle your love. He also focuses on the reasons why couples experience frustration and unhappiness in their love-life.

ORGANIZATIONS:

Concerned Women for America
122 C. Street NW
Suite 800
Washington, DC 20001

Under the leadership of Beverly LaHaye, Concerned Women for America seeks to halt the erosion of the Judeo-Christian moral standards. A $10.00 contribution annually provides the CWA newsletter. The organization has National Prayer Chapter units across the country and an office on Capitol Hill.

Eagle Forum
Box 618
Alton, IL 62002
(618) 462-5451

Eagle Forum is a national pro-family organization which believes the Holy Scriptures provide the best code of moral conduct yet devised and the family is the basic unit of society. A $15.00 membership fee includes a subscription to *The Phyllis Schlafly Report.* Request a publications list by writing the Eagle Forum office.

Free Congress Research and Education Foundation
721 Second Street NE
Washington, DC 20002
(202) 546-3004

The Free Congress Foundation believes that good public policy should foster the traditional family as the basic building block of society. FCF publications, the *Family Protection Report* and *Family Policy Insight* are sent upon request to annual contributors of $25.00 or more for each publication. The Foundation conducts regular training conferences on the techniques of political effectiveness.

Institute in Basic Youth Conflicts
Box 1
Oak Brook, IL 60521
(312) 323-9800

This ministry of Bill Gothard is designed to help families apply basic Scriptural principles to family life relationships and situations. Request seminar schedule and publications list.

Life Action Ministries
"The Family: Holding On for Life!"
Buchanan, MI 49107
(616) 684-5905

This dramatic multi-image production features the Life Action Singers, as well as 2500 color slides and 12 projectors. Write to Life Action Ministries for a schedule, or for information about how to book this production in your area.

Pro-Family Forum
Box 8907
Fort Worth, TX 76112
(817) 531-3605

Pro-Family Forum is a grassroots movement dedicated to promoting the family unit as the vital link in a continuing democracy. The organization seeks to inform people about harmful legislation. A $10.00

membership fee includes a one-year subscription to *Pro-Family* newsletter.

HERITAGE/HISTORY

PUBLICATIONS:

DeMar, Gary, *God and Government: Volume I: A Biblical and Historical Study.* Atlanta: American Vision Press, 1982.

DeMar addresses the battles of lordship—Christ or Caesar (State). The book is designed as a workbook for the reader to apply what he is learning about government, and progresses through church, local, and civil government as viewed from the Scripture.

DeMar, Gary, *God and Government: Volume II: Issues in Biblical Perspective.* Atlanta: American Vision Press, 1984.

Sequel to Volume I. Has a workbook for the reader to make personal application on the material covered in each lesson. DeMar addresses the development of a biblical world view. He devotes the majority of the volume to applying the biblical world view to various areas of life, especially economics and human welfare.

Foster, Marshall, and Mary-Elaine Swanson, *The American Covenant: The Untold Story.* Thousand Oaks, CA: Foundation for Christian Self-Government, 1981.

The American Covenant presents in dramatic and documented language the spiritual foundations of this country. It clearly demonstrates that this nation was founded for Christian and spiritual purposes.

Hall, Verna, *The Christian History of the American Revolution: Consider and Ponder.* San Francisco: Foundation for American Christian Education, 1975.

A compilation of historical documents on the Revolution taken from diaries, sermons, and other extracts.

Hall, Verna, *The Christian History of the Constitution of the United States of America: Christian Self-Government with Union.* San Francisco: Foundation for American Christian Education, 1960.

A compilation of documents showing the Christian influence in the shaping of our Constitution.

Jaspers, Glen and Ruth Jaspers Smith, *Restoring America's Heritage of Pastoral Leadership,* Pilgrim Institute, Granger, IN.

This manual is designed to introduce the individual pastor, educator, or layman to America's Christian history and a biblical philosophy of government and education.

Marshall, Peter, Jr., and David Manuel, Jr., *The Light and the Glory.* Old Tappan, NJ: Fleming H. Revell, 1977.

Traces the providential hand of God in the discovery, establishment, and guiding of our nation. Surfaces little known or forgotten facts about American history.

Walton, Russ, *One Nation Under God.* Old Tappan, NJ: Fleming H. Revell, 1975.

Discusses the biblical principles underlying American society and institutions and how these principles are being replaced by socialistic and humanistic ideologies. What Christians can do to change the trend.

ORGANIZATIONS:

Plymouth Rock Foundation
Box 425
Marlborough, NH 03455
(603) 876-4685

Plymouth Rock Foundation is a major expositor of how biblical principles of self- and civil government offer positive solutions to crucial contemporary issues. It also provides information on America's Christian heritage. A free sample kit is available upon request. Also request the newsletter which covers topics related to the Christian world view.

HUMANISM

PUBLICATIONS:

Hitchock, James, *What Is Secular Humanism?* Ann Arbor, MI: Servant Books, 1982.

A simple, well-written expose' of "secular humanism," this book gives an understandable overview of the cultural shift from traditional, Judeo-Christian values toward a secularistic and humanistic point of view.

Kurtz, Paul (ed.), *Humanist Manifestos I and II.* Buffalo: Prometheus Books, 1973.

Humanist Manifesto I was a result of 34 liberal humanists in the U.S. who in 1933 defined and enunciated the philosophy and religious principles that seemed to them fundamental.

Humanist Manifesto II was drafted 40 years later as an update and more definitive statement by those espousing the humanist doctrine. The Second Manifesto was signed by 114 individuals of distinction and prominence.

LaHaye, Tim, *The Battle for the Mind.* Old Tappan, NJ: Fleming H. Revell, 1980.

Shocking, detailed expose' of the humanist onslaught, as well as a positive, practical handbook for waging war against this subtle infiltration. The author maps out specific avenues you can take to restore God's standards to the institutions and influences that inevitably shape our thinking—and that of our children.

McGraw, Onalee, *Secular Humanism and the Schools: The Issue Whose Time Has Come.* Washington, DC: Heritage Foundation, 1976.

A well documented booklet addressing the erosion of American public education. She knows how values in secular humanism have replaced Judeo-Christian values in American public education.

Schaeffer, Francis A., *A Christian Manifesto.* Westchester, IL: Crossway Books, 1981.

Discusses the biblical imperative for social and political involvement.

Schaeffer, Francis A., *How Should We Then Live?* Westchester, IL: Crossway Books, 1983.

A comprehensive view of the decline of Western thought and culture due to the abandonment of Judeo-Christian ideals for secularism and statism.

Schaeffer, Francis A., *The Great Evangelical Disaster.* Westchester, IL: Crossway Books, 1984.

Traces the how, where, and why of evangelicalism's compromise with secular humanism and liberalism from the 1920's to the present, and explains why evangelical leaders have been so silent and apathetic.

ORGANIZATIONS:

Institute for Creation Research
2100 Greenfield Drive
El Cajon, CA 92021

Offers an alternative to the philosophy of naturalistic evolutionary humanism. Request list of publications and monthly newsletter, *Acts and Facts.*

JUDICIAL SYSTEM/ RELIGIOUS LIBERTY

PUBLICATIONS:

Schaeffer, Francis A., *A Christian Manifesto.* Westchester, IL: Crossway Books, 1981.

This best-seller has become a landmark in the battle for religious freedoms and traditional Judeo-Christian ethics. This is indeed a call to action. What is the basis for Christian civil disobedience? Has the time arrived when Christians should "take to the streets"? This is the most provocative book to date on the subject of resistance to the secularistic trends in our society.

Whitehead, John W., *The Freedom of Religious Expression in the Public High Schools.* Westchester, IL: Crossway Books, 1983.

The title is self-explanatory. Christians involved in work with students in both high schools and colleges must read this book and have it at hand as a most necessary handbook.

Whitehead, John W., *The Second American Revolution.* Elgin, IL: David C. Cook Publishing Company, 1982.

Traces the erosion of the American judicial system from its Judeo-Christian roots to its present state of decline and confusion. Offers a strategy to restore constitutional government.

ORGANIZATIONS:

Center for Judicial Studies
17 Second Street NE
Washington, DC 20002

The Rutherford Institute
P.O. Box 510
Manassas, VA 22110

MEDIA

PUBLICATIONS:

Primer on Access to the Media. Alton, IL: The Eagle Forum Education and Legal Defense Fund.
A handbook designed to assist the ordinary citizen to gain effective access to the media so that all points of view can be fairly represented.

Buchanan, Patrick J., *Conservative Votes, Liberal Victories.* New York: Quadrangle, New York Times Book Company, 1975.

LaHaye, Tim, *The Hidden Censors.* Old Tappan, NJ: Fleming H. Revell, 1984.

Perotta, Kevin, *Taming the TV Habit.* Ann Arbor, MI: Servant Books, 1982.
A unique analysis of television's far-reaching effects on the Christian family. Offers parents practical help for controlling the use of TV in the home.

Schaeffer, Franky, *A Time for Anger.* Westchester, IL: Good News Publishers, 1982.

Details the manner in which secular media and other news-making and opinion-making elites in this country have denigrated and sought to belittle Christianity.

Thomas, Cal, *Book Burning.* Westchester, IL: Crossway Books, 1983.
"Censorship!" cry the Liberals whenever Christians object to a worldview which is being force-fed to an unsuspecting public. But who are the real censors? This book will open your eyes to those who really control what we read and hear.

Winn, Marie, *The Plug-in Drug: Television, Children and the Family.* New York: Viking Press, 1977.

ORGANIZATIONS:

Accuracy in Media
1341 G Street NW
Suite 312
Washington, DC 20005
(202) 371-6710

The monthly *Accuracy in Media Report* points out inaccuracies, distortions, and biases of the news media.

Morality in Media
475 Riverside Drive
New York, NY 10115
(212) 870-3222

Works to stop the traffic in pornography constitutionally by informing parents and community leaders. Operates as a clearing house, researching, collecting, and disseminating information on the problems of obscenity. A newsletter, published eight times annually, is available for a $5.00 subscription.

National Journalism Center
517 Second Street NE
Washington, DC 20002
(202) 546-6561

Offers a 12-week program to train young interns in conservative journalism.

MORALITY

PUBLICATIONS:

Jeremiah, David, *Before It's Too Late.* Nashville: Thomas Nelson Publishers, 1982.
Because traditional values and principles that secured this country's greatness are being ignored, America today faces a danger point. David Jeremiah discusses issues of personal and national concern to evangelicals—and details biblical solutions for immediate action.

ORGANIZATIONS:

Citizens for Decency Through Law
2331 W. Royal Palm Road
Suite 105
Phoenix, AZ 8502
(602) 995-2600

Citizens for Decency Through Law encourages and promotes the publication and dissemination of constructive and positive literature, motion pictures, books, plays, and television and radio programs which possess social value. CDL encourages and supports the law enforcement and prosecution of that which is obscene, lewd, lascivious, and pornographic in these fields of mass communications.

The CDL bi-monthly publications, *National Decency Reporter* costs $10.00 annually.

Freedom Council
Virginia Beach, VA 23466-0001
(804) 420-0773

The Freedom Council seeks to help defend, restore, and preserve religious freedom in the United States. It is committed to prayer, education, and action rather than rhetoric and publicity on a national, state and local level. Their quarterly publication, *The Freedom Report,* is sent to all members.

Intercessors for America
Box 1289
Elyria, Ohio 44036
(216) 327-5184

Intercessors for America calls Christians to united prayer and fasting for the United States, its government, the church in America, and all those in positions of authority. A monthly newsletter is free upon request.

Liberty Federation
305 Sixth Street
Lynchburg, VA 24504
(804) 528-5000

The Liberty Federation seeks to mobilize moral Americans of all religious persuasions to influence government, informs Americans of legislative and bureaucratic plans, and lobbies for positive legislation for a strong and free America. Their monthly publication, the *Liberty Report* is sent to contributors.

National Christian Action Coalition
Box 1745
Washington, DC 20013
(703) 941-8962

The National Christian Action Coalition aims to protect, preserve, and promote the Christian home, school, and church in America. The NCAC's *Family Issues Voting Index,* which rates Members of Congress on ten issues including homosexual rights and private education, costs fifty cents per issue. *The Alert,* the NCAC monthly newsletter, is available for $10.00 annually.

National Federation for Decency
Box 1398
Tupelo, MS 38801
(601) 844-5036

The National Federation for Decency promotes Judeo-Christian values in the media. A $10.00 annual membership fee includes a subscription to the *NFD Journal,* a monthly tabloid newspaper which contains information about television programs and sponsors.

The Roundtable
Box 11467
Memphis, TN 38111
(901) 458-3795

The Roundtable seeks to inform and involve Christian leaders in effective citizenship action. Created for the education and leadership of leaders concerned about national moral issues, the Roundtable's focus is on public policy concerning these issues.

NATIONAL DEFENSE/ FOREIGN POLICY

PUBLICATIONS:

Barrs, Jerram, *Who Are the Peacemakers?* Westchester, IL: Crossway Books, 1983.

A short, easy-to-read biblical exposition that answers the arguments of Christian pacifism. This book deals in particular detail with the misuse made of biblical passages by pacifist Christians, and presents a scriptural viewpoint in relation to issues of war, peace, and justice.

Schaeffer, Francis A., Vladimir Bokovsky and James Hitchcock, *Who Is For Peace?* Nashville: Thomas Nelson Publishers, 1983.

This book sorts out what the whole "peace" movement is about and gives Christians a perspective on questions of arms, war, and the peace movement.

Walt, General Lewis W., *The Eleventh Hour.* Ottawa, IL: Caroline House Publishers, 1979.

General Walt, retired U.S. Marine Corp, writes to alert his readers to the real threat that is upon our own ranks—not external enemies. He basically advocates a two-prong approach. First, the need to purge Congress and the forces of appeasement and surrender which are pulling toward war and famine. Secondly, to replace these Congressmen with men and women of integrity and common sense who will restore our military superiority. He outlines 10 steps for action.

ORGANIZATIONS:

Heritage Foundation
214 Massachusetts Avenue NE
Washington, DC 20002
(202) 546-4400

A public policy research institute which publishes studies on foreign and domestic policy issues. Also publishes the quarterly *Education Update* as well as occasional other materials on education.

High Frontier
1010 Vermont Avenue NW
Suite 1000
Washington, DC 20005
(202) 737-4979

A research organization dedicated to seeking answers in U.S. technology to the strategic problems that plague the U.S. and the free world. The monthly High Frontier newsletter reports on current defense issues.

NEWS/CURRENT EVENTS

PUBLICATIONS:

The Freeman
Irvington-on-Hudson, NY 10533

Monthly, pocket-sized report of sixty pages. Contains information on free-market history, philosophy, and economics. *The Freeman* is available by request without charge.

God's World
Box 2330
Asheville, NC 28802
(704) 253-8063

God's World covers current events in a newspaper for children. It is published on five graded levels (Kindergarten through junior high school). It provides Weekly-Reader-type news reports from a Christian perspective. Write for details about bulk and individual subscriptions.

Human Events
422 First Street SE
Washington, DC 20003

Human Events is a weekly newspaper which supports constitutional government, traditional

Americanism, and traditional values. Subscription is $25.00 per year.

National Review
105 E. 25th Street
New York, NY 10016

This bi-weekly publication is an alternative to the all-pervasive liberal bias of the news print media. The easy-to-read *National Review* gives comprehensive and excellent coverage to news and events, as well as the arts. The subscription is $34.00 per year.

The Phyllis Schlafly Report
Eagle Forum
Box 618
Alton, IL 62002

Published monthly since 1967, *The Phyllis Schlafly Report* has built a reliable reputation for accuracy, analysis, and foresight on education, defense, and family issues. The subscription is $15.00 per year.

World
Box 2330
Asheville, NC 28802
(704) 253-8063

A Christian weekly news magazine, covering general current events from a biblical perspective. Subscription is $23.75 per year (50 issues).

ORGANIZATIONS:

The Free Congress Research and Education Foundation
721 Second Street NE
Washington, DC 20002

Analyzes U.S. House and Senate elections and studies current political trends which have national significance. Also focuses on trends affecting the stability and well-being of American family life.

POLITICAL ACTION

PUBLICATIONS:

Schaeffer, Franky, *Bad News for Modern Man: An Agenda for Christian Activism.* Westchester, IL: Crossway Books, 1984.

Exposes the infiltration of a secular world view in evangelicalism. A call to action and a practical agenda to stop the slide of our culture.

Simon, William E., *A Time for Truth.* New York: McGraw Hill, 1978.

The Intelligent Conservative's Reference Manual. Washington: Human Events Publishers.

How to identify other conservatives, how to run a campaign, how to influence Congress, and the media.

ORGANIZATIONS:

American Conservative Union
38 Ivy Street SE
Washington, DC 20003
(202) 546-6555

The leading political arm of the nation's conservatives, ACU lobbies for conservative programs in Congress and raises funds for candidates. The monthly newsletter, *Battle Line,* comes free with membership. ACU also publishes an annual rating system of members of Congress on social, foreign policy, and economic issues.

Citizens for America
214 Massachusetts Avenue NE
Suite 320
Washington, DC 20002

A grass-roots lobbying and educational organization. Publishes periodic briefing papers regarding current political issues with suggested steps of action. Publications are available upon request.

Conservative Caucus, Inc.
7777 Leesburg Pike
Falls Church, VA 22043

A non-partisan group which attempts to affect policy from the grass-roots level. Publishes voting indexes of congressmen and senators on social issues, available to contributors to the Caucus.

Leadership Institute
8001 Braddock Road
Suite 402
Springfield, VA
(703) 321-88580

Conducts seminars to train young people in political action.

REVIVAL

PUBLICATIONS:

Orr, J. Edwin, *The Fervent Prayer* Chicago: Moody Press, 1974.
The evangelical awakenings of the recent past have a profound influence on the shape and direction of modern Christianity. J. Edwin Orr brings these awakenings out of obscurity and into the important place they deserve.

Roberts, Richard Owen, *Revival!* Wheaton, IL: Tyndale House Publishers, 1982.
Roberts includes historical information on revival, as well as practical guidance in making the effects of revival endure. Written for all those

concerned about their spiritual condition, this book is a clarion call for God's Spirit to move upon His people. A must for everyone longing for genuine revival.

Ravenhill, Leonard, *America Is Too Young to Die.* Minneapolis, MN: Bethany Fellowship, 1979.

In a time when nations all over the world point at America, calling her everything but Christian, the voice of a "minor" prophet once again speaks a major truth: "It is time to quit playing church." The author exhorts modern-day clergy to be prophets instead of puppets, agonizers instead of organizers. In spite of this age of mass communication, he says we are failing to save the contended from the curse of compromise, imitation, and professionalism.

Ravenhill, Leonard, *Revival Praying.* Minneapolis: Bethany House Publishers, 1962.

A challenge to all who are deeply concerned about a full-scale spiritual awakening in America. Ravenhill begins by describing the great need for revival, and then utilizes the remaining chapters to effectively drive home the point. He tells us that prayer is faith in action, and therefore the most essential ingredient in the production of revivals.

Ravenhill, Leonard, *Why Revival Tarries.* Minneapolis: Bethany House Publishers, 1979.

As international politics and economics fast approach the most critical moments of history, one question seems to surface, demanding an answer: Will Christians demonstrate the truth and power of the gospel or will they fold under pressure? This drastic, fearless and ofttimes radical message is meant not only to prevent a decline in spiritual health within the church but also to encourage a single-minded concern within individuals and groups.

ORGANIZATIONS:

Life Action Ministries
Buchanan, MI 49107
(616) 684-5905

Life Action Ministries is a family-centered revival ministry, committed to seeing God give birth to genuine revival among His people, as well as spiritual awakening among the lost. Life Action produced the original multi-image production, "America, You're Too Young to Die," featuring the Life Action Singers.

Other outreaches include revival crusades, a year-round camping program, and revival publications. *Spirit of Revival,* a bi-monthly magazine, is available upon request.

SPECIAL PRODUCTIONS

AMERICA, YOU'RE TOO YOUNG TO DIE.

The television special, "America, You're Too Young To Die," is based on the original multi-media stage production by the same name. The live version of "America, You're Too Young To Die" has been viewed by more than two and one-half million people nationwide since 1980.

The dynamic 75-minute sight and sound presentation features the nationally known Life Action Singers, a computerized visual display with 13 projectors and nearly 2,000 slides projected onto a huge 36-foot screen.

"America, You're Too Young To Die" traces America's Christian heritage, the godly principles on which our nation was founded, and the many blessings God has bestowed on her—blessings which catapulted America from a dependent colony to a position of world leadership in less than 200 years.

The program also documents sobering evidence of the spiritual decline and moral decadence that are subtly destroying our nation today.

"America, You're Too Young To Die" offers a compelling message of hope and solutions through spiritual awakening.

For further information on how you can schedule this live production in your community, church, civic group or organization, please write to:

"AMERICA"
LIFE ACTION MINISTRIES
BUCHANAN, MI 49107
or call toll-free 1-800-321-1538

FOOTNOTES

SECTION ONE
AMERICA YESTERDAY: A NATION ESTABLISHED

One Nation Under God
[1] Verna M. Hall, *Christian History of the Constitution* (San Francisco, CA: Foundation for American Christian Education, 1960), p. iii.

[2] R.J. Rushdoony, *The Nature of the American System.*

[3] Ibid.

Plymouth Rock: A Firm Foundation
Daniel Webster quote: "A Discourse Delivered at Plymouth on December 22, 1820.

SECTION TWO
AMERICA TODAY: A NATION ADRIFT

The Porno Plague
William Stanmeyer quote: Clear and Present Danger (Ann Arbor, MI: Servant Publications, 1983).

John H. Court Quote: *Pornography: a Christian Critique,* p. 75.

The Hidden Holocaust
[1] Franky Schaeffer, *A Time for Anger,* (Westchester, IL: Crossway Books, 1982), p. 117.
[2] Dr. C. Everett Koop, *Moody Monthly,* May 1980.
[3] Ibid.
[4] Bernard N. Nathanson, M.D., *Aborting America,* (New York: Pinnacle Books, 1979), p. 248.
[5] Schaeffer, *op cit.,* p. 160-161.
[6] Ibid., p. 121.

SECTION THREE
AMERICA TOMORROW: A NATION REBORN

Have You Changed Your Mind?
[1] Richard Trench, Archbishop of Dublin.
[2] J. Edwin Orr, "The First Word of the Gospel" (an unpublished essay), 1980.

Priorities and Resistance
[1] Ron Jenson, *Together We Can Deal With Life in the 80's* (New York: Simon and Schuster, 1982).

EDITORIAL CREDITS

SECTION ONE
AMERICA YESTERDAY: A NATION ESTABLISHED

Men Who Paid Freedom's Price
    From "What Price Freedom" by Derric Johnson. Copyright ©1973 by Derric Johnson Press and Zondervan Music Publishers. All rights reserved. Used by permission.

One Nation Under God
    From *One Nation Under God* by Rus Walton. Copyright ©Third Century Publishers, Inc., Washington, D.C.

The Bible and the Dawn of the American Dream
    From *The Second American Revolution* by John Whitehead. Copyright ©1982, Crossway Books. All rights reserved. Used by permission.

Potent Answers to Persistent Prayers
    From *The Re-study of Revival and Revivalism.* Copyright ©1981 by J. Edwin Orr, D. Phil. (Oxford), and Ed. D. (U.C.L.A.). Used by permission.

SECTION TWO
AMERICA TODAY: A NATION ADRIFT

A Nation Adrift
    From *When Free Men Shall Stand* by Senator Jesse Helms. Copyright ©1976. Used by permission of Zondervan Corporation.

Myths That Could Destroy America
    From *Exploding the Myths That Could Destroy America* by Erwin Lutzer. Copyright ©1986. Moody Press. Moody Bible Institute of Chicago. Used by permission.

The Fractured Family
    From *Family Building,* Chapter 2, by Armand M. Nicholi, Jr. Copyright ©1985 Logos Research Inst. Published by G/L Publications, Ventura CA 93006. Used by permission.

The Porno Plague
    From *Before It's Too Late* by David Jeremiah. Copyright ©1982. All rights reserved. Thomas Nelson Publishers. Used by permission.

Is Homosexuality an Alternate Lifestyle?
From *Before It's Too Late* by David Jeremiah. Copyright ©1982. All rights reserved. Thomas Nelson Publishers. Used by permission.

The Hidden Holocaust
From "Deception on Demand" by C. Everett Koop and Dick Bohrer. Copyright ©May 1980 *Moody Monthly.* Used by permission.

Television: The Menacing Medium
From *Together We Can Deal With Life in the 80's* by Ron Jenson. Copyright ©1982. All rights reserved. Here's Life Publishers. Used by permission.

What's Happened to American Education?
By D. James Kennedy. Copyright ©1982. Used by permission.

Freedom of Religious Expression: Fact or Fiction?
From *Freedom of Religious Expression* by John W. Whitehead. Copyright ©1984. Coral Ridge Ministries. Used by permission.

Why Did the Roman Empire Fall?
From *Be Alert to Spiritual Danger.* Chicago: Institute of Basic Youth Conflicts, Copyright ©1979, page 17. Used by permission, January 1986.

The Ruins of Greece
From *Be Alert to Spiritual Danger.* Chicago: Institute of Basic Youth Conflicts, Copyright ©1979, page 17. Used by permission, January 1986.

SECTION THREE
AMERICA TOMORROW: A NATION REBORN

May God Heal Our Land
From *America at the Crossroads* by John Price. Copyright ©1979. Published by Tyndale House. Used by permission of the author.

Have You Changed Your Mind?
From *Loving God* by Charles W. Colson. Copyright ©1983. Used by permission of Zondervan Corporation.

Isaiah Speaks to America
From "America: In a Dark Hour" by Del Fehsenfeld Jr. Copyright © August 1984, *Spirit of Revival,* Life Action Ministries. Used by permission.

Preparing for Personal Revival
From "Preparing for Personal Revival." Copyright ©August 1985, *Spirit of Revival,* Life Action Ministries. Used by permission.

How to Be Sure
Copyright © the Arthur S. De Moss Foundation. Used by permission.

PHOTOGRAPHY/ART CREDITS

America Needs To Return To Its Great Heritage Before It's Too Late. Now You Can Take The First Steps.

America has drifted from its solid foundations. And we've witnessed the alarming results in our society today. Our nation needs a spiritual rebirth—a rekindled walk with God.

It's time to turn around, to get back on course, to rediscover the roots that made America great. And it's not by chance that those roots are found in God's Word.

That's where our roots as individuals need to be too. Because only when we begin to build our lives on God's Word will our nation find its way back home.

But it often seems we don't know how to take the first steps. Life is so complicated. We try to juggle our faith, our marriage, our job, our family. We know what it's like to sigh, "I can't stand the pressure anymore."

You're worried that your kids are drifting in the wrong direction. They're being steered away from the values you consider important. What should you do?

It seems the Bible should help, but it can be hard to understand. And often when we try to read it, we can't get past Genesis!

But if we're ever going to regain our heritage, we must find a way to take the first steps.

We can help you take those steps by sending you a free sample copy of a Bible-reading guide as our gift to you.

The Daily Walk can help you solve life's puzzling questions by encouraging you to read and understand God's Word. If you sense the need to learn how to live God's way in today's world, here is your personal tutor. It will set you on the course to renewed spiritual growth.

Maybe you've wondered how to make the Bible more meaningful to your children.

How can you help them deal with today's tough issues? *Family Walk* will bring your family together as your children learn solid and lasting values from God's Word.

Our nation is made up of people like you. And as you use one of these practical guides, you're taking the first steps toward seeing our nation's spiritual heritage reborn.

Send for your free copy of *The Daily Walk* or *Family Walk* today!

You Can Take The First Steps To Rekindle Your Faith. Send Now For Your FREE Gift.

GIFT CERTIFICATE

Yes, I want to take the first steps to return home to our great heritage. Please send me the free Bible-reading guide I've checked below. I understand there is no obligation. (Please check only one box.)

☐ *The Daily Walk®* for your personal spiritual growth.
  OR
☐ *Family Walk®* for families who want to grow together.

Mr./Mrs./Miss _____
                          PLEASE PRINT

Address _____

City _____ State _____ Zip _____

A-8f

Here Are The Tools You Need To Take The First Steps Home To Our Great Heritage ...

The Daily Walk guides you through the Bible on a practical course designed to bring spiritual growth.

Family Walk builds Biblical roots in young hearts, the future makers of our nation.

... And Here's What People Who Have Taken The First Steps Say About The Daily Walk® and Family Walk®:

"There are no words to describe how much God has used *The Daily Walk* in my life. It is the first time I have ever been able to stick to a Bible-reading program."

"Thank you for this provocative and informative tool to study God's Word. Our children are learning to think and apply God's truth to their lives!"

"I could never complete each day with satisfaction, happiness, and contentment if it were not for the time I take to spend in God's Word with your help."